ENDING ANALYSIS

Gilda de Simone

ENDING ANALYSIS
Theory and Technique

Gilda de Simone

Foreword
Janine Chasseguet-Smirgel

Foreword to the Italian edition
Giuseppe Di Chiara

translated by
J. D. Baggott

London
KARNAC BOOKS

First published in English in 1997 by
H. Karnac (Books) Ltd.
58 Gloucester Road
London SW7 4QY

Italian edition: *La conclusione dell'analisi. Teoria e tecnica*
copyright 1994 by Edizioni Borla s.r.l.

British Library Cataloging in Publication Data

A C.I.P. for this book is available from the British Library

ISBN: 1–85575–126–7

Edited, designed, and produced by Communication Crafts

10 9 8 7 6 5 4 3 2 1

CONTENTS

FOREWORD TO THE ENGLISH EDITION

Janine Chasseguet-Smirgel

This brief, clear, precise, and profound book, beyond dealing with the theoretical and technical questions concerning the termination of analysis, gives a picture of the particular nature of the psychoanalytic cure in relation to the therapies that have come forth from psychoanalytic roots.

Gilda de Simone reminds us that the model of psychoanalytic cure commonly in use today tends to draw away from classical instinct or drive theory in favour of an object relations model. Freud's 1937 paper, "Analysis Terminable and Interminable", is concerned mainly with the patient's conflicts, while the more recent theory—to which the author subscribes—is focused on the dynamic within the analyst–patient couple and on its fluctuations. This latter model, which regards the analytic process as an interaction, tends to efface the asymmetry between its two participants—an asymmetry that is nevertheless fruitful, as witness the analytic setting itself: the analyst on a chair, out of sight of the patient, who is on a couch and is invited to associate freely, thereby being immersed in a regression that is not experienced by the analyst in the same way. Without doubt it would now be useful to integrate the relational model with the Freudian one, which is more reliant on drive theory, as well as with the work of those who take into account the narcissistic regression induced by the analytic situation (Winnicott, Grunberger, and Kohut—the latter unfortunately abandoning the whole of drive theory). Each of these models emphasizes certain crucial aspects of the analytic cure.

Gilda de Simone makes the relational model, which she prefers, work in a creative way. She supports her theoretical reflection with a rich clinical experience. She underlines the problem of separation, which the termination of analysis arouses. All the same, she says that "the experience of separation and separateness could be considered as one of the aims of psychoanalysis". Or one could say that separation straddles the paradigms of drives, narcissism, and object relations.

The author goes on to accord a central role to the experiencing of time. The analytic setting immerses the subject in a timeless universe wherein, simultaneously, time is controlled strictly. The inflexible rhythm (and duration) of the sessions encourages a cyclical conception of time, whereas the feeling of being directed towards a target and an ending produces a linear conception of time. This awareness of temporality is consubstantial with the study of the analytic cure conceived as a *process*. Symptoms and their interpretation in the transference, the idea of change—all of these are themselves conceived from a temporal standpoint. The analytic situation has a "chronopoietic" function. The creation of new temporal forms entails the creation of new symbolic forms. And here we revisit the concept of deferred action [*Nachträglichkeit*].

The analytic process—a function of the analytic situation—restarts a process of frozen growth. The analytic process is not, however, identical with the process of growth. It is from her conception of a dual temporality (the patient being, in some sense, placed into two different orbits) that Gilda de Simone examines the acting-out, as well as the explosion of symptoms and regressive movements, that often accompany the decision to end an analysis: the analytic time that has produced a new order is now abandoned in favour of a different temporality. The transition from the one to the other is the cause of the chaos for as long as the new order is not settled in place.

The emphasis consistently placed here on time and process enables us, it seems to me, to consider more easily the differences between psychoanalytic psychotherapy and psychoanalysis proper. Not that analysis is simply a therapy of greater duration (Gilda de Simone underlines the factors that can lead to an interminable analysis, and also that interruptions in analysis are linked with the existence of unbearable phantasies of interminable analysis), but that analysis allows the use of a working-through process that psychotherapy and its setting only induce to a lesser extent and at a shallower level.

Western man has become impatient. He seems to take as his model the machines that he himself has created, which traverse space and efface time for him. He pushes a button, turns a handle, or works a dial, and he makes his friend a thousand miles away hear his voice, calls up images of Africa before his eyes, boils the coffee, heats the room, and makes it seem as if the treasures of all the world's museums are within range and the most beautiful women are undressing themselves in front of him.

If he suffers from psychic troubles, he believes that, as with an engine, a little oil or some chemical fix will suffice to start things moving again. Perhaps—particularly if the chemical fix does not work—he may submit to psychotherapy, which he will prefer to analysis, which is seen as too long and too astringent (independently of its financial cost). In a way, the difficulties that patients today see in undertaking an analysis are bound up with this general dehumanization. Yet Gilda de Simone's book convinces the reader of the importance of psychic growth and of a deepening knowledge of the internal world which the analytic cure aims to achieve by virtue of its time-bound nature:

How poor are they that have no patience!
What wound would ever heal but by degrees?
Thou know'st we work by wit and not by witchcraft
And wit depends on dilatory time.

[Othello 2. iii. 359–362]

December 1996

FOREWORD TO THE ITALIAN EDITION

Giuseppe Di Chiara

Gilda de Simone has managed to pack into six agile chapters the whole of that vital part of psychoanalytic work that is the theory and technique of the conclusion of analysis. That she can do this with depth and elegance reflects her long career as a psychoanalyst and her specific interest in the subject over the years. Anyone who, like me, has had an opportunity to cooperate directly with the working groups in our psychoanalytic institutes and has followed the progress of Gilda de Simone's research knows full well that this fine book illustrates her ability to coordinate her own experience of psychoanalysis with patients and her exchanges with colleagues at meetings and in teaching—to say nothing of her capacity for thinking things through and communicating them.

A book like this comes at just the right moment. There are plenty of books on general theory and almost too many clinical psychoanalytic case histories, but the same cannot be said of texts on techniques and their underlying theories, even though these are just as important as a basis for practical comparisons and for organizing and disseminating the rules of psychoanalysis.

Gilda de Simone follows current epistemological debates closely enough to know that she is justified in insisting on how difficult it is to formulate any general rules for psychoanalysis. But even so, the scientific foundations of psychoanalysis are solid enough to permit a clear definition of "operating procedures", founded on the basic psychological events that govern psychoanalytic experience. Freud's "Recommendations to Physicians Practising Psycho-Analysis" surely paved the way.

Gilda de Simone appropriately chooses to place the theory and technique of the termination of analysis at the cross-roads where interruption, interminability, and experience of time in analysis meet—a question that has long fascinated her. Her discussion of time is extremely broad-based: she considers the particular status of timelessness of the unconscious, she discusses and reflects on the different forms of "temporality", using the term to mean a sense of time, looking at the specific time-patterns of each patient, and she roves widely among the writers—Flournoy, Ricoeur, Meltzer, and the Barangers—who have dealt with the topic. Naturally, she also ponders the question of linear and cyclical time and inevitably returns to the subject of *Nachträglichkeit* [deferred action] and the parallel between the termination of analysis and the events of loss, mourning, and death.

The author sets great store by Freudian *Nachträglichkeit*, viewing it as capable of breaking the linear continuity of processes by uniting past and future. But at the same time she easily allows for the fact that in every analysis there are also linear segments of process and of time. With the same spirit of objective criticism she discusses the general isomorphism between psychoanalysis and other experiences and segments of life, excluding too close a connection between the termination of analysis and painful loss, while leaving open the question of the type and number of points in common—theoretical and practical—between life and analysis. What seems certain is that, during analysis, time-modes are formed, with all their consequences: on the one hand, interruptions and interminability; on the other, the conclusion of successive vital cycles. The same thing happens with other experiences.

Research into psychic interactions is highly productive, both in analysis and elsewhere. With regard to time, for example, just think of the importance of experience and how it is achieved and illustrated by the parent who promises a child an explanation "when you are older". Thus, the analyst's mental attitude—already implicit in the rhythms of analysis—suggests that, however important it is, however intense it may be, it will eventually come to an end.

This book discusses the criteria for ending analysis in all their depth but not at excessive length. Some of these criteria are solidly acquired and corroborated by experience, while others are still uncertain and need further testing. This comparison starts already with the reader and the writer: why not, for example, plan for termination at the beginning of the holidays, as my patients and I often, though not necessarily always, do?

It is in the concluding phase of analysis that we need to look back at one basis for evaluation discussed right from the first lines of this book: there are, of course, criteria for terminating analysis that are proper to and characteristic of the psychoanalytic experience, differently formulated in time, from the amplification of the Freudian ego to introjective identifications with enrichment of the most recent inner equipment. However, we must not forget the starting conditions and motives that induced us to begin the analysis. We must remember the capacity to heal the psyche, common to psychoanalysis, on which we must also confront each other and which—with other elements—governs the conclusion of analysis. This conclusion is as varied as the psychopathologic pictures with which it may start.

Very appropriately, emphasis is laid on the fact that psychoanalysis can cure or at least improve a person's mental condition. This is already a great deal, but fortunately it does not create supermen. Imperfect conclusions serve to remind us of the difficulties in our work; not only do we have obvious limits, but we also have a long way to go.

Difficulties in ending analysis can show up mistakes made while it was in progress, unexplored resistances and defences, inadequate ordering of countertransferences—and the author's own experience on this subject illustrates these points well—but they can also place us squarely within our own limits, the limits of our knowledge and our technique.

Talking about the conclusion of analysis means talking about self-analysis—its possibilities, characteristics, and limits. The last chapter of the book looks at that part of the psychoanalytic experience that is carried on when the analyst is no longer present. Gilda de Simone has examined this issue on other occasions, not hiding her doubts about the possibilities of self-analysis. Among the difficulties of the termination of analysis there is the possibility, first observed by Abraham in narcissistic pathology, of a "sort of pseudo-self-analysis".

This type of defence may arise—I must agree—but I also consider it important to be aware of the self-analytic progress the patient is completing, especially in the concluding phases of a successful analysis. In my experience, one can see how the patient himself, having achieved a correct self-reflective observation, leaves it preconsciously uncompleted, leaving room for the analyst to add something of his own. Once analysis is finished, this capacity for self-reflection will be the fulcrum of what we call self-analysis.

It is certainly true that the conscious mind can only reflect on the preconscious events that become conscious when it finds itself in that mental condition we call the depressive position. As an aside, it comes to mind how much we have still to learn about this brilliant intuition of Melanie Klein's, so often misunderstood through her misleading and imprecise naming! Gilda de Simone mentions it, as does Lyda Gairinger, who discussed this subject so well. Before this mental condition we can only—as Bion taught us—be patient, tolerating frustration and pain. How is a well-conducted analysis useful to us in this? I believe that this is the most important fruit of a psychoanalytic therapy, and the basis for a lasting healing capacity after the analysis, though the extent will differ from subject to subject and according to life's circumstances.

These few introductory words are certainly not enough to do justice to the richness of this work; every time we go back over it, we find new facets of the problems, a wealth of new arguments, and important suggestions for research. This book is destined to take its place among the basic texts on the subject of the conclusion of analysis, besides being a brilliant example of psychoanalytic writing. I want to express my pleasure at having had the privilege of introducing it with these few lines.

PREFACE

This book, in which I have returned to and amplified the topics covered in my previous works about timing in relation to the termination of analysis, grew out of my need to tackle the question afresh in a more organic way, and at the same time to link it with the new ideas stemming from my clinical experience.

The order of the chapters corresponds to when and how various questions cropped up in my clinical practice.

The first question is one that every analyst must ask himself at the very outset: is analysis terminable? And if so, how and in what sense?

In the attempt to find answers, I have let my interest range over questions of timing, theoretical and clinical models, techniques, the problem of difficult conclusions, and the huge variety of themes connected with the post-analytic phase.

I do not intend to review all the vast literature on the subject, but interested readers will find, at the end of the book, in addition to a Reference section, a Bibliography of works of general interest and references to authors not directly cited in the text.

The much-discussed question of the criteria for ending analysis thus pales in comparison with the importance of collecting, throughout the course of analysis, the events of the assumption of the sense of time and of separation.

The book is addressed especially to colleagues in clinical practice. I hope, however, that it will also be useful to anyone who, for whatever reason, is studying psychoanalysis and wants to see the theory brought to life through the description of the step that I consider best illustrates the complexity and potential for change of the analytic experience.

This clinical and technical question—how does an analysis end?—thus opens the way to innumerable issues bearing on questions of mental health, treatment, healing, and knowledge.

ENDING ANALYSIS

CHAPTER ONE

The elusive criteria for ending analysis

Any discussion on ending analysis is closely interwoven, or even virtually at one, with the aim of analysis. This is immediately clear from the vast literature on the subject where any one author, even while declaring his model of the termination of analysis, is in fact usually referring to his own theoretical and clinical model of psychoanalysis in general.

We must clearly take into account the close links between the final phase of an analysis and the situation at its beginning: the level reached at the end cannot be viewed separately from that at the beginning, so it is not always possible to expect the same level of development for different cases. Naturally, the question of "analysability" arises here—which cases does a particular therapist accept or refuse? Just as each analyst's criteria for analysability are fairly specific, so are the criteria for termination. For example, the interruption of an analysis whose course had been predictable from the start cannot be equated with one presenting all sorts of foreseeable difficulties and changes in technique.

It is only in relation to an initial plan that we may conclude that we have arrived or not at an adequate conclusion. But what plan is adequate for psychoanalytic treatment? Even without separating the start- and end-points, many transformations can occur that may lead to unexpected or unforeseeable results.

The interlinking of the two themes—the ending and the aim of analysis—helps explain our difficulty, and sometimes uneasiness, in the face of admittedly praiseworthy attempts to formulate "criteria for the termination of an analysis". As I have already pointed out, these are often simply a direct reflection of each author's own theoretical and technical model.

In *The Fundamentals of Psychoanalytic Technique* (1986), Etchegoyen notes on several occasions that, from the theoretical point of view, the criteria for ending analysis relate largely to each author's concepts regarding disease, the therapeutic process, and the cure. Sometimes—and here the greatest caution is necessary—they relate to personal visions of the world and even to ideologies.

Often the criteria for ending analysis reflect the corresponding conception of mental health. The universal example is the now famous set of criteria set out by Rickmann in 1950, to establish the *point of irreversibility*—meaning the point at which the process of integration has reached a level that will be maintained after the conclusion of the analysis. To summarize, these points are: the elimination of infantile amnesia and the working-out of the oedipal conflict; the achievement of heterosexual supremacy; the capacity to tolerate frustration and one's own aggression without excessive guilt feelings and without losing object-love; the capacity to work through mourning.

These criteria clearly relate to a concept of mental health. They reappear, without substantial differences, in the works of many other authors, and in a certain sense they can still be considered valid, though today, in my opinion, we have some difficulty in accepting the notion of a *point of irreversibility*, because of our greater awareness of the continuous and inexhaustible possibility of change.

One of Etchegoyen's concluding observations is certainly worth bearing in mind: it may well be true that the concepts of the factors in the therapeutic process and the cure vary with different schools and authors. In reality, though, if we examine them without preconceptions, we can find points of agreement, and in the consulting-room there is a surprisingly wide consensus with regard to the assessment of a patient's progress.

All bibliographical references to the ending of analysis come naturally from Freud (1937c) and from Ferenczi (1927), who was Freud's inspiration, setting the pessimism of the former against the optimism of the latter. Balint (1936), too, had a model of a "new beginning", with the transformations of primary object-love, and Klein had her concept of the need to work through paranoid and depressive anxieties; then, too, there is Rickmann, who has already been mentioned. A. Meotti, who read a paper on "The Termination of Analysis in a Historical Perspective" to the First Italian–German Congress at Loveno (1991), also cites the models of Money-Kyrle, Jaques, Winnicott, Kohut, and Rosenfeld.

As we continue with the description of the various models, we get further and further away from the instincts model and nearer to the relational one. Consequently, the aims of analysis—and the criteria for its termination—no longer coincide only with the solution of drive conflicts and defences, or overcoming paranoid or depressive anxieties, or acquiring a good arsenal of internal objects, but the accent shifts onto the formation, structuralization, and amplification of the self.

Freud himself used various models, depending on the stage of development his theories had reached. We pass from the initial formula (1916–17), in which the aim of analysis seems to be to attain the capacity to work and love, to a formula for making the unconscious conscious, and from there to the famous assertion: *"Wo Es war, soll Ich sein."* His paper, "Analysis Terminable and Interminable" (1937c), is well known for having raised the question of resistance to analysis and cure. Here Freud did not directly pose the question of transference and countertransference, nor that of mourning and separation—all of which were, on the other hand, to characterize the conceptualization of modern theoreticians.

Thus in the decades separating us from Freud's 1937 work, the history of ideas on this subject can basically be divided along two main lines: one concerned with the patient and the solution to his conflicts, the other—more recent—concerned with the patient–analyst relationship and the transformations that arise within it. By and large, therefore, there is a long series of authors, including Freud and Ferenczi, who refer particularly to the patient and who tie the satisfactory conclusion to treatment to the solution of the initial conflicts.

Later, and especially in the last few years, the emphasis has shifted more and more from the patient to the analyst and to the analytic couple at work, and to a concern with contact and separation; this emphasis has also been embraced by Italian psychoanalysts (Barale & Ferro, 1992; Bezoari & Ferro, 1992; Di Chiara, 1992; Nissim Momigliano, 1974, 1979, 1992a, 1992b).

It is worth remembering the conclusions proposed by A. Meotti (1991): "In general terms, Freud's *'Wo Es war, soll Ich sein'* and Bion's *'reality has to be been'* still seem to indicate the aims of analysis best, precisely because in their abstraction and simplicity they sound the most detached from theories and systems of values in competition and historical succession." The task—and the difficulty—lies in establishing a stable contact with external reality through internal reality.

Also pertinent are some remarks made by G. Maffei and colleagues in their paper on the criteria for the termination of analysis (1992). Referring back to Ticho (1972) and his work on "treatment goals, life goals", they note that there is often a certain degree of confusion between the goals of analysis and life goals. This is a valuable argument against the danger of idealizing analysis, since, when this happens, it inevitably works against analysis itself. We are therefore well advised to draw a sharp distinction between the two, because the patient will only be able to conclude the analysis properly if its goals are seen in clear relation to their limitations and their difference from the goals of life; only then will the patient be in a position to take advantage of analysis to attain his life goals.

Referring especially to the works of the early period, we find that many questions concerning the technique for ending analysis seem complicated and hard to answer, precisely because of their partial viewpoint. It happens sometimes that the analyst is dissociated from the patient, so that the ending of analysis becomes a question regarding only one of them—for example, questions such as who is to decide, when and how to communicate the "decision" to the patient, what changes to make in the setting, how to overcome the patient's resistance to the analyst's decision. All these questions are directly related to the patient's dissociation from the analyst, a plan for termination taking shape in the mind of each of them independently.

Klein, too, goes into the matter in her paper, "On the Criteria for the Termination of a Psycho-Analysis" (1950). She proposes as a criterion the complete working-through of persecutory and depressive anxieties, with the aim of putting the patient in the best position to work through the mourning for the ending of analysis, and she concludes: "Moreover, when we decide that an analysis can be brought to an end, I think it is *very helpful* to let the patient know the date of the termination several months ahead" [italics added].

Basically, this assumption of a "unilateral decision" on the part of the analyst is of the same nature as the attitude that impelled Freud to the "heroic measure" of fixing a time limit for his analysis of the Wolf Man and that subsequently led many analysts, faced with an *impasse*, to imitate him. I think that today very few analysts would share this view; the prevailing idea now is more that the conclusion of the analysis concerns not only the patient and the modification of his personality, but the whole relationship between analyst and patient, because of what it means in the transformative development of the subject.

From this point of view, the most interesting thing is the mode of transformation of the analyst–patient couple, so any criteria can only be formulated within that relationship. I therefore agree with Grinberg (1980), who proposes that the "decision to separate" is the result of a process that has operated during analysis in both the patient and the analyst. This brings to the foreground each particular analyst's countertransferential components, his theories, and his models of technique.

I would therefore suggest that *it is impossible to formulate a general theory on the ending of analysis or any all-embracing criteria valid in every situation. In just the same way, general theories on "interminability" or "interruption" are not possible.* This, of course, does not mean that we cannot find developments or passages on which to build a model that will fit a large number of cases; despite the obvious relativity of the criteria proposed, we cannot avoid working to find concepts on which to reach sufficient agreement.

I shall therefore reformulate here—as I have already done several times in the past—a first suggestion: *there is no general technical and theoretical problem of "how" and "when" to conclude a treatment, and the specific problem is really how and when to work through—or really disclose—phantasies or thoughts on the termination of analysis.*

In every analysis there are moments when the element of "separation" emerges and is worked through. It is as well to specify at once that here the term is understood in the dual sense of "separation" and "separateness", the first indicating the possibility of separating oneself from a real object, the second referring to differentiation (Di Chiara, 1978; Quinodoz, 1991). The more we experience separateness, the more we shall be able to experience real separation.

Di Chiara (1978) suggests a description of separation in terms of "an element of psychoanalysis": "Separation allows sensual gratification to be replaced by thought, or by the capacity to think thoughts, but also to 'dream dreams'—the capacity for introjective identification and the capacity to remain alone." Separation also guarantees the birth of responsibility. Wittgenstein, in his "Notes on Frazer's Golden Bough" (1931), says that "the awakening of the intellect takes place with a separation from the original soil, the original foundation of life". This is a very suggestive idea, and I like to imagine the analytic process punctuated by these *awakenings of the intellect*. The experience of separation and separateness could be considered one of the aims of analysis.

These fertile opportunities in the analytic process emerge in various ways in individual cases. There is therefore a new or even an unheard-of acquisition of a sense of time in the form of experience of one's own time, the time of the analysis, and the time of life. This assumption of one's own time is expressed through manifest or latent thoughts on the conclusion of analysis, often with phantasies of interminability or interruption. Often, in fact, a phantasy of interruption may be interpreted as a phantasy of interminability or vice versa (de Simone Gaburri, 1982a, 1985, 1990b).

These are the moments when the transformative processes, which will blossom at the appropriate time in the actual plan for termination, start up—or are blocked. One must be careful not to let them pass by, so they do not look like lost opportunities when viewed with hindsight. Nested within these phantasies, in fact, we often find hidden what we can recognize as the personal aims of analysis of that patient.

These moments point to the passage between two different ways of perceiving time in the analytic setting. I have always laid much importance on these phantasies of interminability and interruption, because it seems to me that, given the time-mode of the analytic setting, the patient often struggles for a long time with the dilemma of opposing temptations when facing the idea of dependence: to submit or to avoid it. The analytic setting comprises apparently contradictory attitudes towards time: on the one hand, there is a sort of unwritten code not to worry about the passing of time and the duration of the treatment; on the other hand, we move within a context of strictly controlled space and time. There is thus a sense of timelessness evoked and controlled by the setting itself.

In these moments of the analytic process, which I mentioned at first, there is an assumption of a "personal" time, and I think this is a useful point for the development of the sense of identity. According to the theoretical model from which we started, we can speak of the "threshold of the depressive position" (Meltzer, 1978) or of the "oedipal cross-roads" (de Simone Gaburri, 1985), or of the emergence of the separation element, as many writers suggest (for example, Quinodoz, 1991). It may otherwise be a question of drawing on resources that have remained unexpressed, bogged down, to structure a more creative self. In any case, we are touching upon a focal point that marks the beginning of the path towards termination. This is the point at which, together with this "personal" time, we begin to perceive the conclusion of the analysis as *thinkable*.

At such moments the destiny of the analytic process is often at stake: analyses are frequently interrupted at this point, or else a tendency to interminability begins to show itself. In most cases, however, the movements that will lead to an adequate conclusion begin here. It is worth stressing that these events occur at these "nodal" points of the process, and sometimes even very early on, not at the end of analysis. It is in this sense that *we cannot speak of the criteria for the ending of analysis as a matter arising when we "decide" to conclude an analytic treatment*. Interminability is not a question of the ending of analysis; it is a problem regarding each single analytic process—a problem whose preliminary signs have perhaps been misunderstood.

In my previous writings, I quoted from Winnicott's work "The Aims of Psychoanalytic Treatment": "In doing psychoanalysis I aim at keeping alive, keeping well, keeping awake. . . . Having begun an analysis I expect to continue with it, to survive it and to end it. I enjoy myself doing analysis and I always look forward to the end of each analysis" (Winnicott, 1962).

The call to be alive, healthy, and awake indicates what the analyst's mental state must be, and at the same time the state into which we want to bring the patient, as one of the goals of analysis. Winnicott also seems to suggest that one of the aims of treatment is actually to end it, which means giving the patient the opportunity to experience "separation".

This new or renewed acquisition of the sense of time can thus be expressed directly through the discovery of one's own personal time. This will be familiar to anyone who perceives that "time exists" or that "so much time has passed", to anyone who discovers the sense of transience or decides that it is "time for change". A patient once said: "I always wanted to have babies, but I see now that I was always thinking of very small babies, and it is only now that I come to think of a baby growing up. . . . I realize that until a while ago I believed that you, too, thought of me this way, and that you were not interested in making me progress with the analysis and bring it to a conclusion."

Another patient refused, among other things, to acknowledge the passing of time, to the point that when she was obliged to declare her age, she would reply in mathematical riddles from which her age could be deduced only through the addition and multiplication of very small numbers. This patient said one day that until then she had never noticed that the flowers in the analyst's room were wilting and needed to be renewed. "You are betraying me", she said. This patient had the utmost difficulty in taking decisions appropriate to her age, causing herself serious damage, obviously fostering the illusion that she still had plenty of time left to decide what to do "when she grew up".

Phantasies on the ending of analysis, as I have already said, may take the form of phantasies of interruption or interminability, and every effort is needed to understand the patient's own urgency so as not to let oneself be distracted by the manifest content. Often, a treatment perceived as interminable actually ends by being interrupted; and one seen as a phantasy or acted-out interruption may mask strong anxieties relating to an idea of interminability. For a long time, some patients will not allow themselves to accept the setting, with its implicit state of dependence, because they are too anxious about remaining prisoners of a situation that is beyond their control. People who are having this experience use expressions such as: "I have the impression that my analysis is just beginning now" (after analysing the phantasy of interminability and even after deciding on the conclusion); "I'm glad you have made me understand that analysis can finish"; "Now that I can think about termination of the analysis, I'm happier to continue. . . . I no longer feel it needs to end urgently"; or even, "Now that I know that the analysis will end, I can really begin".

A typical case is that of a patient who, after several years of analysis, announced his intention of breaking it off. He felt he had made enough improvement, and, despite some residual difficulties, he thought that therapy could not help him any more. In fact, he was disappointed, because the treatment had not produced the change he had expected at the beginning, when he had hoped to "change radically". It was possible to discern a phantasy of interminability beneath the idea of interruption, and, beneath the project of "radical change", a phantasy of magically omnipotent transformation, which in reality left intact the actual defensive adjustments that were harming him, but which he did not want to give up. Basically, this was a case of what is often called a "perverse contract" of the type: "I am having analysis so as not to change", unless it is a magically omnipotent solution (de Simone Gaburri, 1981; Usuelli Kluzer, 1989).

This was one of those patients who said, after some time: "My analysis can begin now." He also added that he had gone back to painting a panel he had begun years earlier and had then interrupted—a sort of triptych, entitled, "The Ages of Man". When he had originally stopped painting it, his plan had been: "I shall finish it when I am near death." Now he had changed this to: "I shall finish it when I am ready to stop analysis."

As we shall see in a later chapter, it may happen that an analysis is considered as interminable or interrupted only because it does not conform to too rigid a plan or is only held by the patient or the analyst, or both in different ways. We shall return to these themes and to the analyst's countertransferential implications.

Clinical experience shows that this intertwining of phantasies often arises in patients who are reproducing the ways in which the sense of time—especially the difficulties of managing time personally—had appeared initially. One patient, at a moment when these phantasies were emerging, said: "Today, coming to the session, I thought of the end of analysis. I imagined you would say to me one day, 'Now we've finished'. I would want to carry on, but you would make me give up. Other times I have thought that you will never let me go . . . that you will always want to control my life." The phantasy of a tyrannical analyst with regard to time was grafted over an image of parents who had always called her "our little woman", not "our child"; who had never told her fairy-tales, because they considered them "frivolous and childish", and who had never accepted "childish chatter". On the other hand, these parents had always been present to check her progress at school and work, spurring her on to do things "faster and faster", but at the same time trying continuously to interfere in decisions because it was only then that she became "our poor little girl", who needed them and was incapable of doing anything on her own.

In connection with plans for terminating the analysis, this phantasy of a tyrannical possession of time by the analyst is frequent, though often not manifest; frequent also is the phantasy of an analyst who cannot himself tolerate separation—like a parent who always needs his child to be a baby, never a grown-up. A patient only manages to get out of this *impasse* when he succeeds in coming to the conclusion that the parents themselves feel gratitude to their child not only for being born, but also for growing up satisfactorily.

One patient had lost her parents in adolescence and lived with the feeling that her parents had cheated her of the possibility of paying them back for the time they had devoted to her and for their "sacrifices": "I won't have the chance of being the prop of their old age", she said. She felt that she had not loved them enough in her childhood, and now the only solution was to remain a child forever and offer her time to her parents. She did this by putting off all possible choices of adult life and by completely unruly behaviour in analysis with regard to punctuality, attendance at the sessions, and fees. The patient, in other words, was acting out the phantasy of repaying the analyst in the same coin as she was receiving—that is, her time—so that on the one hand she wasted her time, and on the other she nourished a phantasy of interminability, offering the analyst "her whole future". In her phantasy the analyst had come to a sort of pact-with-the-devil with her: "I, the analyst, give you my time, and you give me your soul in exchange, and you will never again be separated from me."

This patient finally escaped from the *impasse* and agreed to a plan for ending analysis when she was able to accept that it was not obligatory for anyone to pay their parents back with the same amount of time they had spent looking after them in their childhood.

In addition to the above ways, which specifically involve a sense of time and timing, the idea of ending analysis may appear on the analytic scene under other guises: it can, in fact, come to light in innumerable ways. Variables that come into play are the subject's personality, the way that particular analytic process is proceeding, and the phase of analysis in which this idea appears.

Very often we recognize an element that was presented at the beginning—a dream, a symptom, even only a word, or figures typical of that patient's personal mythopoiesis. Liberman (Liberman et al., 1985) attempted a more precise scheme of these signs, which he calls *indicators of the ending of analysis*. He speaks of *temporal indicators, indicators of movement and detachment, and indicators of typical personages*. Often the recurrence bears the signs of a transformation that has taken place: the words and dreams indicate a different meaning, and symptoms increasingly acquire the value of communication. Etchegoyen (1986) notes that Liberman also spoke of *linguistic indicators* in the sense of the acquisition of complementary styles and a greater mastery of language. Guiard (1977) even suggested an indicator reflected by changes in the musical component of the patient's language.

We need only go back to Freud and the Wolf Man to see that near the termination of analysis, or when it is proposed, symptoms, phantasies, thoughts, and memories often become acute again. Problems we thought had been overcome re-emerge, and new thoughts and difficulties may even appear. Sometimes these are the outlet for resistance to the planned termination; at other times they are a sign that further working through is still needed, when faced with the real prospect of separation. In yet other cases they indicate the situation already described—the re-acquisition of parts of the personality that had been kept hidden up to that moment, or a readjustment to transform the "separation", spurred by the emergency.

This is an important moment, which gives great momentum to the sense of identity, when three basic elements of the analytic process work together; urged by a real idea of "parting", the sense of "meeting" between the analyst and patient may be reinforced, and the "telling" also assumes new expressive possibilities, to use Di Chiara's terms (1992).

From this moment on, the idea of the termination has entered the analytic stage, even if it is not manifest or continuously in the mind of the patient and the analyst. In fact, it should not be. I agree with those (including Grinberg, 1980) who hold that it is better if the idea of termination is not continually present in the analyst's and analysand's minds, so as not to put obstacles in the way of the analytic process. I believe that what the analytic couple will feel—though not necessarily manifest—is the acquired perception of time.

We shall come later to the real concluding phase after deciding *when to terminate*, and, as we shall see, much water has still to pass under the bridge.

CHAPTER TWO

Time in psychoanalysis and the concept of the psychoanalytic process

If the conclusion of analysis is a feature to be borne in mind throughout the whole analytic process, not only near the actual end, we need to reflect on how the patient's phantasy-related events unravel as he discovers—or re-discovers—and develops a sense of time.

The first part of this chapter follows the progress of the sense of time in analysis; in the second part we seek to understand what meaning we can give today to the concept of analytic process.

It is not possible here—and perhaps not useful either—to go back over all that has been said about the sense of time in psychoanalysis: Freud's first famous assertion on the lack of time sense of the unconscious, the birth of a sense of time in relation to the oral and anal stages, the temporal perspective in relation to object frustration, hallucinatory anticipation, connections with the events of the depressive position and the oedipal constellation, cyclicity, linearity, continuity and discontinuity. I shall do no more here than hark back to or suggest some concepts that seem to me useful for this discussion.

In the analytic setting we see a sort of polarity between a lack of time sense in the direction of regression and a new discovery of the sense of time tending more in the direction of transformation and the project. In a previous work (de Simone Gaburri, 1979), I suggested thinking of interpretation as if it were an "event" that contains the past in the present and is open to the possibility of new transformation. I believe this is why a successful interpretation may involve "discovery", "surprise", "marvel", but also "recognition".

As I said in chapter one, the analytic setting embodies a sort of contradiction that is one of its constituent elements: on the one hand there is the rigid rhythm that promotes regression and seems to reflect a cyclic pattern, and on the other the undeniable sensation of proceeding towards a final goal—a conclusion. Thus, within the analytic relationship we find the dialectic terms of linearity and cyclicity that have always occupied the minds of thinkers in discussions of the concept of time.

The ambiguity and bipolarity intrinsic to the setting set the pace between phantasy and reality, between *hic et nunc* and *alibi et tunc*, which underlie the intertwining of the continuous with the discontinuous (Sacerdoti, 1986).

Certain of my patients indicate how they perceive time in the analytic setting (de Simone Gaburri, 1979):

P1: "In this room I feel as though I were in a space with walls, like an amoeba . . . things are worrying because I don't know where they come from or where they are going . . . the sensation of being jammed in, shelved in one place, just a number . . . too fixed a time and space, almost suffocating . . . I am afraid time may stop here."

P2: "I am afraid of letting myself go on this couch as in a cradle: minutes, hours, days pass over me like seasons."

P3: "Here everything is like a caricature—the pace, the set times. We could be in a temple with a Buddha who need not even speak. Basically everything can flow into an underground life parallel to the real life, and the two lives might never meet: a time and a space that govern themselves alone . . . you've just got to get used to the idea, to the pace. Sometimes I think that the analyst could be dead, and one could carry on talking and it would not make any difference."

P4: "I want to ask you: wouldn't it make sense to concentrate the sessions—a lot of very long sessions each week, getting it all over in a few months? Why this lack of continuity, these pauses, this going on without a limit?"

P5: "You are the master of time. If you did not exist, I would not have come here . . . it is as if you had asked for this analysis, not me."

These are some of the things we may be told, especially at the beginning of treatment, that indicate a regressive shift.

At the other pole, the projectual one, we must catch the point where the possible transformations of a past, which is no longer an obligatory memory, converge with the future, which is no longer an omnipotent procrastination. The analyst must free himself and the patient from the double temptation to use memories as mechanical objects and to plan the patient's future for him.

I have tried in the past (de Simone Gaburri, 1982b) to think of the time of analysis as being fenced in between symptoms and knowledge. I thought of the symptom as a sort of encapsulation of emotive situations that remain outside the process of development and the flow of transformative experiences. I talked about "a congealed clot of time" or even "parasitic time" which takes up energy without giving anything in exchange, its elements remaining cut off from the developmental process. I frequently quoted a patient who described this situation, relating it to his own history, in symbolic words:

"Periodically I found myself in a world where I couldn't understand whether it really had anything to do with me . . . and life seemed like a roundabout, a closed ring in which my father, my mother and I played tag without ever managing to touch or stop each other . . . my father never managed to touch my mother, my mother never managed to touch me, and I could not touch my father and make him stop."

This situation recalls the one described by Fachinelli (1979) on the subject of obsessional patients, in whom "there is an immobility fixed in time and space which is defended, we might say, through Zeno's arguments". He refers to the paradox Zeno of Elea used to demonstrate that time did not exist. Action is not carried out in time because time is divisible to infinity; the arrow shot from the bow only seems to move—in reality it remains motionless at its starting point.

These characteristics of "immobility" suggest an image of the mind, while a symptom is building up, being flooded with the emotions that have caused it, and thus remaining paralysed in a state of immobility. From the point of view of the temporal order, the symptom is therefore a *compulsory step.* Analytic work can thus be considered as the quest for *alternative pathways.* When the symptom is communicated and can thus be analysed, it is already showing its intention to be transformed, so it has partly lost its ability to cause paralysis.

When the analytic process starts, it develops a temporal course substantially different from the everyday rhythm of life. Its temporal qualities are such that it comes to constitute a sort of deviation from everyday time: it carries the patient on a trajectory with its own space–time coordinates. This orbit, in which the analytic process proceeds, cannot and should not coincide with the time of everyday life—except temporarily and partially. Only at the end, when analysis is reaching a conclusion, and sometimes only after the conclusion, can the two orbits gradually draw together to the point where the one in which the analytic process is going on disappears, or meets up again with everyday time.

In the analytic setting a constant balance must be kept between two tendencies drawing towards opposite poles: the regressive tendency and the progressive tendency. Grinberg et al. (1967) use an expression that gives a good idea of the opposition and interplay of the two tendencies and how their two trajectories circle separately. If it is true—they say—that the process indicates progress, it is also true that regression and progression do not follow the same direction in real time and in analytic time. Kris spoke of "regression in the service of the ego", and we are led to speak of "progression in the disservice of the ego"—as happens, for example, in flights into recovery, in hasty solutions to symptoms, and so on. This is a *parting of the ways*, therefore, between the direction of the symptom and the direction of the process.

What we call the *hic et nunc* in which we operate is thus this whole unstable situation, so it is not just this moment and this place, but means experience, and hence knowledge, of all the paths traced by these progressive and regressive shifts. We thus reach a situation in which the two parties may find themselves simultaneously in the same orbit, depending on this particular time created in the relationship. I have spoken of the same time—*simultaneousness*—not of the same situation—coincidence—in the relationship; in fact it is the symptom itself which, by interrupting the developmental process and freezing an emotive situation, represents the satisfaction of the need for coincidence, for bringing into the present that past which—to paraphrase Racker's words—"never really became past". In the relationship—that is, in the present—this past loses its ability to freeze the situation as soon as it is interpreted in the transference.

In the relationship between analyst and patient, the symptom acquires a meaning as communication and may lose that foreign-body feeling it had had previously. Flournoy, in his book *Le temps d'une psychanalyse* (1979), mentions the specific time in which the analyst meets the analysand in the present, calling it "secondary time". Flournoy holds that the symptom is formed with no regard for the time needed, and time is involved only in its paradoxical aspect of "timelessness". The solution of the symptom in the relationship, on the other hand, involves time in that achieving it takes up that secondary time that is neither "not the sense of time" nor everyday time, but is midway between the timelessness of the unconscious and the function of the analyst, setting time because it "separates". This secondary time finishes with the termination of analysis.

We have therefore put the symptom outside the "disease–cure" system, so it can regain its meaning as a "sign". The changes made to the meaning of speech/symptoms—changes arising in the time-context of the analytic relationship—create an *eccentric* experience that provides an alternative to the primary communicational rigidity of the symptom. This explains the importance in the analytic relationship of any state of mind related to separation, solitude, or even surprise and wonder; all these situations help to sustain the germinative power of a changing mental state, which needs this experience of an outer ring beyond the everyday routes of life and the "concreteness" of events. It will therefore be possible to identify the time-course followed by meaningful, progressive speech. The sequence of these moments, in fact, is what constitutes the specific analytic communication and the knowledge on which transformation is based.

All this has a basic relevance to the theme of the termination of analysis. At the conclusion, in fact, the patient must not only give up the pathological parts of the self and modify the relations between the self and objects, but must set up an internal movement that progresses through the acquisition of changes of meaning in the frame of particular space–time sequences. The acquisition of this type of knowledge does not refer to theories or explanations; to have experienced analysis does not at all mean that one has theories about psychoanalysis—something which, in fact, often reveals a purely defensive aim. This is precisely because of the space–time coordinates in which the event is lived, with analytic time and real-life time in eccentric orbits.

"In analysis we cannot avoid the clash and collision between two times: external time, which is suspended, and internal time, which exists during the sessions", says L. Russo (1991). This is a correction of the phenomenological argument that does not admit the simultaneous presence of two times, whereas the analytic setting not only admits it but needs it. Another correction arises from the fact that from the very outset of the analytic experience the intersubject relationship is a groundstone of the temporal experience, and "only in the relationships between two minds is it possible to find the specificity of the temporal dimension". The subjective origin of the idea of time coincides with identification with the other, which is at the same time "object of and obstacle to desire".

In the analytic experience renewal is constant—the fresh discovery of the sense of time; therefore, the analytic situation has a *chronopoietic* function. This invention of new time forms coincides with the genesis of new symbolic forms.

All this is connected with another, widely shared idea: that time becomes human time to the extent to which it is expressed in a narrative, and the narrative reaches its full sense when it becomes a condition for the acquisition of the sense of time (Ricoeur, 1983).

In the work to which I refer, Russo lays much stress on *Nachträglichkeit* [deferred action]—a concept that has been justly re-evaluated in recent times and is very important for our discussion of the termination of analysis and the concept of the psychoanalytic process (Baranger, Baranger, & Mom, 1983; Di Chiara, 1991; Modell, 1990; Riolo, 1986; Thomä & Cheshire, 1991; Thomä & Kächele, 1985; Usuelli Kluzer, 1992). Freud uses the term *Nachträglichkeit* as part of his concept of a sense of time and psychic causality: he means that every psychic experience is repeatedly re-worked in the light of new experiences and access to a subsequent stage of development. Laplanche and Pontalis (1967) noted that this conceptualization excluded even then that summary and rather ingenuous interpretation according to which personal history is determined linearly through the action of the past in the present and leads to the mistake of thinking of human destiny as being played out entirely in the first phases of life.

More specifically, the concept of *Nachträglichkeit* expresses the fact that new experiences enable us to work through again anything that had not been placed in a significant context—for example, a traumatic event. This re-working-through is stimulated by new events or by the achievement of a new level of maturity. The main component is the step-wise time pattern typical of man's development. The true basis of a sense of time lies in the conflict between prematurity and the confrontation with the other that impels the subject to climb the uneven steps from one level of development to the next. All this starts from the basic idea that the infant, premature by definition with regard to his drives, is characterized by lack on the one hand and expectation on the other. At each new stage of development, one way of temporally conceiving experience gives way to a new temporal experience being created.

Le Guen, in his *Après-coup* (1982)—the French word for *Nachträglichkeit*—defines it as a moment of re-acquiring meaning that causes a break, the discontinuity that ensures continuity. This concept, which enabled Freud to reconcile the apparently irreconcilable dichotomy between the linear time of consciousness and the timelessness of the unconscious, enables us to reconcile the continuous with the discontinuous and is very important here for the theme of ending analysis and for the concept of the analytic and post-analytic processes.

The concept of *Nachträglichkeit* thus interrupts linear continuity by interweaving the past with the present and future, to the point where Freud casts doubt on whether real memories of childhood do in fact exist or are made up: "A doubt fundamental to the development of psychoanalytical thought" (Usuelli Kluzer, 1992).

At this point we must look more closely at the concept of the psychoanalytic process, which is no less problematic and variously understood. As for its history, with its present meaning it was lacking for a long time in the works of Freud and his successors. It dates back in fact to 1966 and the Pan-American Congress in Buenos Aires, when it came definitively and gloriously onto the scene, destined to play a pivotal role in psychoanalytic conceptualization. A broad definition has it as a sequence of events that are taken into consideration as they happen within a situation called the psychoanalytic setting, through the analyst–patient relationship.

The first question is whether the events—or at least some of them—are isomorphic with the events of growing up. Two main concepts stand in opposition here: the first has it that the process is natural and isomorphic with the facts of growing up, and that the tendency to transference is natural. The second, however, considers the process as having been created by the analytic situation, and that what happens is not spontaneous and automatic but depends on the interaction of the two subjects involved.

My suggestion is to think of the process as created by the analytic situation, not isomorphic with the events of growing up, but setting in motion again a growth process that had stopped or remained blocked at some points. The analytic process may not be natural in itself, but we can consider that the potential for progress that it re-establishes is natural.

I think we should beware dwelling too much on the analytic process as creative, since this may give rise to idealization or illusory constructions, although we are probably justified in thinking that in the end creativity will be released, possibly making itself felt only after the conclusion of analysis.

Meltzer (1967) certainly made a more complete attempt to describe a linear, natural psychoanalytic process in recognizable and foreseeable steps that would be applicable to every case. I agree that today it is not possible to use this sort of model, which is in danger of being used like an instruction manual, with an excessive *a priori* emphasis on the objectives to be attained and on the concept of integration, which creates idealized objects—not ideal ones. However, as I said in chapter one, some of Meltzer's "passages" still seem useful and significant, and are presumably a part of every analytic process: for example, "the threshold of the depressive position", which I believe represents in many cases that particular moment of analysis when we see the re-acquisition of a sense of time, together with other transformative movements.

Meltzer (1967) says:

> The threshold of the depressive position is a turning-point in the economics of mental pain in the analytical process, when the waning of persecutory anxieties gives way to the waxing of the depressive position. . . . Each step deeper into the depressive position, with its shifts from self-interest to concern for the objects, brings more urgently the realization of both the dependence and the eventual weaning.

I believe that every analyst experiences those "turning points"—real stepping stones throughout the course of analysis—at which, as I said in chapter one, the patient's phantasies relating to terminability and interminability develop. On the other hand, I do not agree with the use of the term "weaning", because it seems too closely bound up with the growth model, and because I feel that the "decision to detach" involves a much more polyhedral situation, comprising various levels.

The model of the passage from the paranoid–schizoid position to the depressive position is also increasingly seen—especially by Bion—no longer as a set of progressive steps in an obligatory linear dimension, but as mental constellations balanced among themselves that are never really overcome. The "oscillation" model illustrates this well, suggesting that the moments of integration attained can break up at any time and give rise to new regroupings and transformations. In fact, the two positions—paranoid–schizoid and depressive—which are usually viewed as two steps towards maturity, come to represent a general way of functioning of the mind in the oscillation model (Neri et al., 1987).

The analytic process, then, is not a means for re-working through the past in pursuit of a project already outlined; it is more of an attempt to break down the sediments and mental blocks that the subject is keeping within himself, so as to reach new meanings and symbolisms. Nevertheless, it is unquestionable that anyone experiencing the analytic situation has in their mind the image of a linear segment of time with a beginning and an end. Breaking it into distinct periods is useful in making us aware of time, and also makes the facts conceivable.

The psychoanalytic experience has an undeniable chronopoietic function, as we have seen. Human time—based on an irreversible progression towards death and occupying a position somewhere between the irrecoverable past and the unknowable future—cannot fail to break up the cyclic pattern. Then, too, the idea of death—"the insight into death", so to speak—is not related to the end of life, like an interruption or termination, but stands more "at its shoulders": death begins from that "remnant of the infinite indetermination of the sense which we call *identity*" (G. Marramao, 1991). This also explains why, at the moments when there is a re-adaptation to the sense of time and finiteness, the feelings that emerge are not discouragement and desperation, but quite the contrary—we feel a sense of fullness and potential creativity, precisely because a first step has been made towards the acquisition of identity.

However, I repeat that I do not think that the time of analysis can be considered as isomorphic with that of life, which would lead to excessive emphasis in the concluding phase of analysis on the elements connected with loss, mourning, and death.

At this point, I can most usefully refer to W. and M. Baranger, some of whose ideas are basic to our discussion. The Barangers, too, lay great stress on the concept of *Nachträglichkeit,* which allows the reconstruction of the present and its classification as history in relation to the past, and they maintain that analytic work involves the "invention" of new emotive situations, which can then be "historicized" so as to acquire a sense of continuity. To quote them:

> The session . . . is the optimal experience for the direct observation of the genesis of a sense of time and history. The analytical process in some measure rewrites the subject's history and at the same time changes its meaning. The moment in which we observe this change, in which the subject simultaneously re-assumes a piece of his history and opens up his future, is the moment of "insight". Analytic work takes place in the here and now and in the past, in the dialectics of the closed and repetitious temporality of neurosis and fate,

and the open temporality of *insight.* [Baranger, Baranger, & Mom, 1983]

I find this way of looking at analytic work very pertinent: it considers a reciprocal action between regressive and progressive tendencies and suggests that the effect of a successful interpretation is to get the patient out of the state of timelessness of unconscious phantasy current at that moment, giving new meaning to an item of the past and opening up a new perspective. Thus there re-emerges a conflictual element, which changes with its context and produces new events, which, in their turn, act on the earlier ones.

Once again, we see that the interpretation of an event is never definitive and can always be amplified by new elements: in the best cases, one reaches a conjunction of emotive facts integrated in the interpretation, which wipes out the conflictual element at the root of the symptom.

The Barangers also place great emphasis on the importance, in the production of these phenomena, of the ambiguity of the temporal dimensions in the analytic situation. They speak of the contradiction between admitting that the process takes a regressive direction while at the same time maintaining that the unconscious is unaware of a sense of time. They conclude with the suggestion that regression might be considered as a product of time versus timelessness, and that the ambiguity of the analytic situation is particularly propitious for this.

It is, above all, this possibility of reorganizing the events of the past on the basis of new relational experiences, giving them a new meaning, that explains the therapeutic utility of the symptom, once it can be placed in a narrative. Leaving aside the convention of the linear influence of the effect of the past on the present and the present on the future, here, too, there is an "oscillation" between *Anlehnung* and *Nachträglichkeit,* between the repetition of the past in the present and the new significance of the past dictated by the present. The conflicts of continuous and discontinuous, of structure and history, of repetition and reconstruction, are thus integrated and resolved (Le Guen, 1982; Riolo, 1986).

M. Baranger (1969) distinguishes between a "genetic sense of time" and a "technical sense of time". While "genetic" time, that of development, is linear and remains within the theory of the complementary series, technical time—created in the setting—is born of the meeting between analyst and analysand, and the analyst's intervention is not an added factor in the complementary series. It can only be understood through conceptual categories such as situation, integration, insight.

However, in any discussion of whether the analytic process is "natural" or "unnatural", we have to beware of carrying our points to extremes. As we shall see in a later chapter, we always find a focal point persisting in the patient, regardless of what the analyst does. Thus I believe I can close this part of my subject using Di Chiara's suggestion (1990), in the preface to the *Treatise* of Thomä and Kächele. Di Chiara says that while perplexity or even refusal to use a "strong naturalistic model" is more than understandable, there are also some points that favour a "weak naturalistic model". This would not be so weak as to be founded only on personal facts inherent in the analyst and patient and, though weak, would not be caused by but "linked with natural processes like the growth of the natural skills of human beings, of their interrelational instrumentation and their biological vicissitudes". Di Chiara means a nature that is weak and disorientated but "original and deep", with a valuable though fragile potential that can develop on the basis of relations and social events.

Psychoanalytic operations hinge around the basic nuclei of this "nature", within the analytic dyad, where they can acquire new expressive capacities.

CHAPTER THREE

The concluding phase of analysis

Let us now imagine ourselves in the concluding period. We are about to part from our patient. We look back on our mental attitude towards him, how this analysis was similar to others, and in what respects it was unique. What change has there been from the beginning? How much was predictable, and how much unforeseen? What phantasies do we now have about the post-analysis stage, if any?

All this is summed up in the basic question: do we really need a particular technique to conclude an analysis? In this chapter we try to answer this question. Are changes in the setting necessary in the concluding phase? Who should fix the date for conclusion—the patient or the analyst? These technical questions have been widely debated, especially in the past. As I have already said, when speaking of the relational model that I have adopted, I am convinced that in the majority of cases the patient and the analyst can arrive at a decision together, so as a rule there seem to be no particular problems specific to this moment.

We find ourselves agreeing with Freud (1937c):

> We must first of all decide what is meant by the ambiguous phrase "the end of analysis". From a practical standpoint it is easy to answer. An analysis is ended when the analyst and the patient cease to meet each other for the analytical session.

This may seem tautological, but shortly afterwards Freud adds:

> *The other meaning of the "end" of an analysis* is much more ambitious. In this sense of it, what we are asking is whether the analyst has had such a far-reaching influence on the patient that no further change could be expected to take place in him if his analysis were continued. [italics added]

And in a later chapter, after suggesting that not only the therapeutic analysis of the patient but also the personal analysis of the analyst is transformed from a "terminable task" into an "interminable task", Freud (1937c) immediately goes on:

> At this point, however, we must guard against a misconception. I am not intending to assert that analysis is altogether an endless business. Whatever one's theoretical attitude to the question may be, the termination of an analysis is, I think, a practical matter. Every experienced analyst will be able to recall a number of cases in which he has bidden his patient a permanent farewell *rebus bene gestis* [things having gone well]. . . .

Berenstein (1987) also specifies that

> Psychoanalysis is *interminable* because it deals with the unconscious and the mental world. However, psychoanalytic treatment is *terminable* because someone—the patient or the analyst, or both—has to terminate at some time, when both agree, or do not agree in the case of a unilateral decision. But in this case the relevant word is *"termination"* and not *"terminable"*.

However, things are never quite so straightforward, as the vast amount of literature on the subject shows. I am convinced it is because of that "other meaning of the expression *end of an analysis*" that Freud mentions in the passage quoted. In fact the argument on technique has become an attempt to discover the best conditions for reaching the most satisfactory conclusion.

If we go over the literature once again, we note all the questions that come up most often: who is to decide the date of the last session and when, whether it is conceivable or even, in certain cases, advisable, for the analyst or the patient to decide unilaterally; how far in advance the date should be fixed; whether from that moment we should make changes to the setting, whether the analyst should change his attitude; and many more such questions.

I think the concluding phase of analysis begins when the patient announces that he wants it to end, and this time the analyst feels that his wish is not a thing to be interpreted, but that he has to answer the patient. This is the meaning of the expression *acte de passage* [act of passage] which Flournoy (1985) uses to designate this moment, as opposed to *passage à l'acte* [acting], a term we would use to define in other conditions any reply of the analyst on the plane of reality. We shall come back to this shortly.

Once it is established that a conclusion is possible, there will be a period in which the patient's anxieties relating to separation will emerge; there will be turbulence, with the appearance or reappearance of symptoms, states of resistance will come to light, but one more step will be made in the direction of the patient's own identity.

In my opinion, setting the date of the last session is best left to the patient. As the concluding phase progresses, the patient will fix a date—first approximately, and then he will indicate a definite day. I agree with all those who affirm that, once fixed, the date of the last session should not be changed, except in exceptional circumstances. I also agree that changes in the setting—for instance, in the number of sessions—are neither necessary nor advisable, so as not to dilute the emotive impact with "separation". For the same reason I prefer not to schedule the end of analysis to coincide with normal holiday dates. I also agree with a point Lipton made years ago in his work, *The Last Hour* (1961): he maintained that even in the very last session a new situation might arise, calling for the working-through and interpretation of conflictual elements that had eluded us until then. This confirms the advisability of not changing the setting—especially the analyst's "mental setting".

Naturally, there are cases where changes are indicated, but they should stem from a very precise need of the patient, not of the analyst. The apparent simplicity of the situation described, however, does not mean that problems will not crop up; many interesting observations are still to be made.

In the first place, this is a period marked by a real paradox: analysis ends just when it has become most creative and pleasurable, and this situation may pose considerable problems to the patient and the analyst in the sense that resistance may develop to the separation, with emphasis on the elements of mourning and loss.

There is also a second paradox: in this phase, having even scheduled the exact time of the ending, we must try to continue work as before, without thinking too much about ending, so as to preserve intact our capacity for working through and interpreting any elements that, as we have seen, can re-emerge in this phase. Grinberg (1980) recommends insistently that in this concluding phase we proceed "without memory and without desire", as Bion puts it.

Flournoy examined the question of the "decision" in great detail. The *passage à l'acte*—inevitable at this time, when the analyst has to answer on the plane of reality—becomes the *acte de passage,* which is, in fact, the title of his book (Flournoy, 1985). At a certain point—Flournoy suggests—there are signals that herald the ending of analysis, which are recognizable by their special status: they can no longer be referred to the transference nor interpreted, but demand an answer on the plane of reality:

> It will be thanks to this particular status that the analyst will be able later to think that the arguments based on these signs, which lead to the ending of analysis, were neither arbitrary nor insignificant, even if they could never be justified in analytical terms.

We are speaking of an act—a decision, not an interpretation—that implies leaving the analytic process and setting. This is an *acte de passage* towards a time that is different from the secondary time of analysis, yet it also moves towards a rediscovered time that is at once equal to and different from that which had preceded the beginning of analysis, when the secondary time was first established.

All this concerns only the moment of the decision and the agreement between patient and analyst; subsequently, in the actual concluding phase, it is best that nothing in the setting be changed, particularly the analyst's mental attitude. We must, as Etchegoyen specifies, be aware that the concluding part has begun "formally and strictly".

In many cases, especially in patients particularly sensitive to the mobilization of the affects concerning separation, the *acte de passage*—that is, the exit from secondary time—appears very directly in the clinical material: either actually in the session, or often in dreams, it appears as a disruptive and sometimes catastrophic event—the breaking of a barrier or a plate of glass, a leap into the void, leaving for or returning from an interplanetary journey.

I remember a case in which the subject, in a dream, was piloting a space vehicle and had to re-enter the space–time of the earth, but he no longer knew what type of operations he had to carry out—addition, subtraction, or division. Another subject was at the wheel of a car in a landscape that had become deserted, but he lost control of the car, which zig-zagged rapidly forwards, backwards, and sideways. One patient who had difficulty in fixing the date for the last session said: "If I could choose how to die, I would choose to die in my armchair, talking to a friend . . . an end to my life in which everything would happen simply, naturally."

It has long been known—beginning with Freud and the case of the Wolf Man—that fixing the conclusion date livens up the patient and makes him much more productive, culminating in a return to, or a new explosion of, symptoms or regressive movements. This happens especially if, as in Freud's case, it is the analyst who authoritatively fixes the date (which today we think should not be done), but also if the decision is made by the patient himself. The exit from "analytic" time, which re-proposes a new spatial and temporal order, produces disorder before the reorganization. However, the decision to conclude must be more of a "selected act", to use Bion's term, than a *fait accompli* (Gaburri, 1987).

But—as we said—things do not always go so smoothly. Some patients try to shift the responsibility for the decision onto the analyst alone, and to make him "act" in that direction. Here the whole range of resistances to separation becomes evident. In some cases the date of the final session is fixed, but then the patient seems to forget it, only to remember it a short while before the end.

Quinodoz (1991) noted that this last attempt at splitting or denial can be worked through even at the very end, and it has a special place in the history of subjects with separation problems. Sometimes the difficulty in fixing a date corresponds to the phantasy of being able to put it off until the last minute, creating a *fait accompli* rather than a selected act—like that patient, quoted above, who said, "Basically my wish is to die in an entirely natural way, in my sleep or during a conversation with a person dear to me, without warning and without suffering", and ended with: "I can fix a date if I can do it only a week before." Some subjects put themselves in the position of being *obliged* to decide by some external event.

The phenomenology is very vast, and virtually everyone is a unique case. Quinodoz devoted a whole book, *The Taming of Solitude,* to this subject, with exhaustive case-histories. He maintained that solitude could be "tamed" by the working-through of separation anxieties. From this analytic work will emerge the feeling of "buoyancy" that is the acquisition on the patient's part of independence and the capacity to be alone, which urges him towards creative transformations.

What I said earlier also remains fundamental: in the concluding phase of analysis, the setting of the session and the analyst's mental attitude must remain unchanged. In this period, separation anxieties often occupy the greater part of the field and have to be worked through; the more the patient has already acquired a sense of *separateness,* the easier it will be to work through them and overcome them.

Since I adopt the relational model, the stress laid on the countertransferential components will be easy to understand. I have already spoken of the indispensable state of alertness to pick up any movements that might be "precursors" of the conclusion or indicators, according to other authors, as we have already seen in chapter one.

Only approximate indications can be given on the question of when it is appropriate to decide on a conclusion. Even a very long analysis can be considered as interrupted, and a much shorter one as concluded. Klauber specifies, in his "Analyses Which Cannot Be Terminated" (1981), that long analyses have to be clearly distinguished from interminable ones, and that often interminability is just a name given to a particularly difficult analysis. It can also happen that an analyst considers a treatment interrupted or interminable in relation to a model he had in mind *a priori,* and if he suspects that the treatment is tending towards interminability, he must look back over what has happened up to that moment, and whether by chance he has not colluded with some phantasy or resistance of the patient.

In a previous work of mine I illustrated this type of situation with a clinical case to which I should like to return here (de Simone Gaburri, 1985). It concerns a patient who after many years of analysis seemed to be slipping towards interminability. Despite evident progress on the personal and social levels, the patient did not show the slightest sign of wanting to consider conclusion unless—he said—"some particular event arises". The analyst was almost resigned, and often had the idea of advising a change of analyst so as to get out of the *impasse* and conclude the analysis.

The patient had had the idea of suicide several times in the past, and even now, giving various justifications, he kept a revolver in his bedside table drawer, and would repeat—jokingly, it seemed—"What does it matter if I don't manage to solve my problems, or if things go badly? The revolver is always a way out."

One day the patient arrived dressed differently from his usual style, more "casual". He said he was irritated and worried about the business he was running, but above all he was bored. Then he said that at a certain meeting he had met a friend and learned that he was suffering from a fatal disease. No one seemed to bother about it, not even the sick man himself. Our patient said he felt different from others, more conscious of the evils of the world, less likely than others to deny them. He said he had seen his father and his mother die and be buried, and now he would be upset to see the burial of this friend, who was younger than himself and had always been healthier, both physically and mentally. "It's all so depressing", he said, "this time I shall really have to shoot myself out of it."

The analyst perceived for the first time the possibility of a different meaning to the patient's expression—that is, to get out, not in the sense of killing himself, but in the sense of deciding to get out of this situation. The analyst felt gripped by a strong emotion, a mixture of dizziness and fear, as had happened when he had learned that the patient—who, among his other symptoms, had a severe vertigo syndrome—had begun to practise a very dangerous sport.

The patient continued by telling him that another friend of his, a rival at work, had lost his influence, and this would allow him carry out a project this friend had opposed. He added that this would be possible because the rival, despite being clever and healthy, had always remained firmly and rigidly attached to old-fashioned attitudes: he did not realize that times had changed and that it was no use pretending things were still the same.

The analyst, as though speaking of himself, then remarked that now it was possible to overcome the dizziness caused by the idea of the unknown, of changes and choices. It was conceivable that even the analysis, too, could end . . . perhaps the fatal disease was really the idea that this was not possible without acknowledging that times had changed.

After some time, the date could be fixed, and the analysis concluded adequately (from later notes, in fact, it appeared that the patient was able to progress further). Thus, the analyst had let himself be caught within a state of dizziness, of numbness and fear for the patient, which prevented him from working through the double meaning of the expression "I shall shoot myself out". The patient's progress—the cure of the dizziness and the new sport—were seen as dangerous for the patient. His competitor, ousted from his high position because of his inflexible attitude, was that part of the analyst which had colluded with the part of the patient that had always been convinced they could be separated only through a process of interminability/ interruption. The "I shall shoot myself out" in the sense of "I am killing myself" was equivalent to saying: I am separating myself according to a process of interminability/interruption.

In the second sense of "shooting himself out", a separation can occur at the very moment when a meeting is created through the discovery of a new meaning. The analyst "wakes up" (in the sense indicated by Winnicott, cited earlier), so a relationship can be established for a phantasy that the patient had up to then imagined only as a break and interruption.

Clinical experience, we repeat again, especially that concerning re-analysis, shows that often an analysis has been considered to be "interrupted" or to have the characteristics of "interminability" only because it did not correspond to an initial project that was too rigid or unilateral on the part of either the patient or the analyst. A project that has been somehow mapped out in advance by one of the two, in fact, often leads the patient to a "perversion of the transference" or the analyst to a "perversion of the countertransference" (de Simone Gaburri, 1981). I believe that the root of many so-called interminable analyses and many interruptions of analyses can be found here. In many cases this amounts to what Usuelli Kluzer (1989) calls a "perverse contract".

In chapter four we look more closely into these questions of resistance to the conclusion of the analysis.

Having arrived at this point, we could recount and review all the innumerable ways in which the last sessions of an analysis may run; but this would need a whole new chapter. I shall just note a few points I consider highly significant.

Unquestionably, in the last phases the patient tends to push both himself and the analyst towards a certain type of acting-out. I think we must resist this temptation, without becoming inflexible, so as not to lose the last precious and sometimes unpredictable opportunities for working through. Often the last recurrent themes have to do with the experiences of death, or birth, or rebirth. However, I have also heard patients comparing the end of analysis with a marriage rather than with birth or death. A woman patient said in the last session: "I am happy and full of emotion, but a little lost. Like at a wedding. Saying 'yes' means separating oneself from so much of one's own past life". *Rebus bene gestis,* there is always the feeling of having acquired the capacity to take on new tasks.

It is possible to study the features of dreams in the terminal phases and detect phantasies about the post-analytic phase (Ferrara Mori, 1993). In analyses that end well, there is often the feeling of an emotion that seems to consist of a sort of acquisition of beauty, in the sense of enjoying a rediscovered harmony between the self and things. A patient who had been tormented for a long time by the idea that the analytic procedure was absolutely non-scientific, and thus not productive, said in one of the last sessions that he was surprised to find himself marvelling at the sunrise for the first time. "But it is so comprehensible an event, almost banal and insignificant!" he said to himself, and yet he felt that he was opening up to the possibility of new knowledge (Gaburri & de Simone Gaburri, 1982).

At any rate, in all cases that conclude adequately, there are simultaneously feelings of loss and detachment, including regrets and nostalgia, as well as the desire to move on to other creative possibilities. A patient said at the moment of conclusion: "It is like after the School Leaving Examination . . . it was what I wanted, I got it, in fact it went very well, but I wasn't completely content—I thought I had left something out, I would have gone back inside to look at it all again, but I knew I couldn't do that—I knew it was time to turn the page."

CHAPTER FOUR

Difficult conclusions

In "Analysis Terminable and Interminable" Freud sought to understand what there is to hinder the good termination of an analysis, rather than what facilitates it. This is one of the reasons why this work gives such an impression of pessimism.

We too must now consider the factors that hinder an adequate conclusion, always keeping in mind the basic concept I keep stressing—namely, that these are not just specific problems related to ending analysis; they happen to be more directly noticeable when a project for conclusion is expected but resistance comes to light. Even interminability is a concept that does not just concern the end of analysis; it concerns all those situations that prevent us from progressing towards the conclusion.

That is why I agree with Etchegoyen (1986), who prefers to speak of factors that impede the psychoanalytic process. He singles out *acting out, negative therapeutic reaction,* and *reversible perspective* (meaning an attempt to overturn the analytic situation, moving it in the opposite direction). Acting out acts on analytic work, negative therapeutic reaction on the results of that work, and reversible perspective on the analytic "contract". In other words, the first puts action in place of thought, the second annuls insight, and the third goes directly against the project for transformation by attacking the bond and the emergence of the psychotic part of the personality.

To these three concepts, I would add that of *perversion of transference*, which I consider appropriate to keep separate, and I shall explain why.

Acting out, or at least a tendency to do this, is very frequent in the concluding phase of analysis as a defence against separation anxieties and grief at the loss. We can still follow Grinberg's elaboration of this in his paper to the International Congress in Copenhagen (1967), in which he brought to light the root of acting out in primary mourning that had not been sufficiently worked through. Pain not worked through is reversed upon the analyst or outside the setting, or even in the body, giving rise to somatic symptoms. All this is exacerbated at the end of the analysis, and here the danger of collusion on the analyst's part is very strong, because he finds himself caught between his own task of elaborating the detachment from the patient and the temptation to ally himself with him to avoid suffering. A modern approach to the factors hindering an adequate resolution of analytic treatment sees the concepts of acting out, unshakeable resistance, negative therapeutic reaction, and perversion of transference combined: the *impasse* merits a place on its own.

Freud, to explain these states—which he saw mainly as negative therapeutic reactions—resorted to the concepts of sense of guilt, masochism, and even the death instinct. Many investigators since have interested themselves in these problems, and interpretations have multiplied. Today we prefer to speak not so much of the patient's specific pathology and the analyst's mistakes in technique as of these ways of expressing, through action, emotional areas still far removed from the possibility of being represented or thought, especially in relation to traumatic situations that have not yet been worked through. There may be a defensive stance against a state of awareness that causes pain and was at one time indicated by the expression "resistance to cure" or "risk of being healthy". These phenomena are in fact not easy to distinguish, and it would be a mistake to tackle them according to a rigid model and then try to validate it in clinical practice.

Abraham, in his short but extraordinary work of 1919, "A Particular Form of Neurotic Resistance against the Psychoanalytic Method", already describes these complex phenomena almost completely when he intuitively uncovers the basic fact that the patient, on account of his narcissism, cannot admit the analyst's role and, though apparently very willing to carry on with the analysis, has in fact to invalidate the analyst's interventions and authority.

Abraham notes that some patients refuse to follow the rule of free association. They speak as though they already had preset ideas they are not willing to give up. At first sight they give the illusion of being very open towards psychoanalysis, but resistance lurks behind this apparent docility, a hidden defiance of the analyst, who is seen as a father/authority figure. The only feelings these subjects communicate are those in sympathy with their ego. They are humiliated by the facts that come to light during the analysis but do not fit in with their pre-established aims. Abraham speaks of the *narcissism* of these patients and also touches on the topic of envy—these patients refuse dependence and are convinced that they can do everything on their own.

One further point—very important in my opinion—concerns another situation we see so often: outside the session, these subjects tend to do things they would never consent to do in the session. They arrive thus at a sort of "self-analysis", a mental pseudo-activity in the absence of the analyst, which becomes a sort of masturbation, for which they feel no guilt since it is justified and even "prescribed on therapeutic grounds" (Abraham, 1919).

We see sketched here all the elements that we must discuss concerning obstacles in the way of the analytic process and its conclusion. How can we now classify Abraham's intuition? A negative therapeutic reaction, a reversal of the perspective, or perversion of transference?

The *impasse* merits a separate discussion. We can call it an undercover, insidious attack on the normal course of the analytic process, meaning that it corresponds to an unconscious phantasy of paralysing the object/analyst by following a perverse/cryptic project. Certainly this begins with the patient, but it ends by involving the analyst, sometimes totally. There are no recognizable technical errors, no visible resistances, nor changes in or attacks on the setting (Etchegoyen, 1986; Maldonado, 1983). It may all lead the analyst to ask himself at a certain point: "How did we get here? What happened that I failed to notice?" Unfortunately, in some cases it is too late to regain control of the situation because the patient is slipping inexorably towards a situation of interminability/interruption.

There are no clear-cut boundaries between these various situations. For example, a negative therapeutic reaction may have a positive effect in that it may indicate a misunderstood *impasse*, as Barale and Ferro suggest (1992) in a work with a very significant subtitle: "A Too Clear-Minded Analyst, a Too Perfect Patient, a Misunderstood Impasse."

It is essential to bear in mind, as Etchegoyen asserts on several occasions, that these concepts are technical, not psychopathological, even though in many cases the connection with elements of psychopathy and characteropathy is automatic. I believe that there can be no doubt that the *impasse* and the phenomena connected with it are a disease of the relationship, if for no other reason than the deep and sometimes total collusion induced in the analyst. It is better not to get involved in the sterile arguments about "who started first" that try to place the responsibility entirely either on the patient's psychopathological structures or on errors and weaknesses of the analyst (Ferro, 1993). Both these positions may have the effect—or even the aim—of evading the effort of understanding the analytic facts that are really taking place in the here and now.

However, we must also beware excessively stressing the purely relational facts, because that could diminish the importance and the patient's responsibility for his internal emotional facts, which predispose him to such a radical attack on the analytic work.

One of the most insidious and destructive elements is in fact the idealization of the relationship with the expectation of a "happy ending" resting on almost total denial. I have often met this in persons who have already undergone formally successful analyses but who were now asking for a new treatment. In some of these subjects the idealization persisted to the point that they were unwilling to reveal the previous analyst's name; some declared that in no case would they allow their former analyst to be told that they had felt the need for subsequent treatment.

Even in cases where the patient's character defect is obvious, the analyst must nevertheless persevere with his task. Here I disagree completely with those who theorize on the practical necessity of the "heroic" expedient (in Freud's footsteps) by acting out changes in the setting, going as far as interruption. In my experience, these methods—though they do sometimes unblock the situation—basically induce a compliance in the patient, based on denial of aggression: the patient submits, but then, without saying a word about it, goes and puts his complaints to another analyst.

I agree, on the other hand, that the analyst is bound by the very nature of his work to the hypothesis that resistances can be overcome and all forms of mental pain alleviated, and that any failure remains such and cannot be overcome through extra-analytic expedients. Being convinced of the need not to make any exceptions to one's own responsibility to the patient is the best safeguard the analyst has against his own counter-transference, which can harm the patient (Meltzer, 1968).

On the subject of the "heroic expedient", a term coined by Freud and widely adopted, why does the adjective *heroic* concern the analyst's actions, while for the patient we talk simply about acting out or interruption? As Sarno (1984) points out, the adjective "heroic" should also apply to the patient, because of his ability to overcome resistance to analysis and its attendant suffering, and to tolerate or even encourage separation. Sometimes the interruption instigated by the patient is the only weapon against a stalemate situation beyond the analyst's control.

What means do we have available to overcome these situations, which impede the analytic process and make it difficult to conclude? The answer is almost tautological: to persevere in our work, not to allow ourselves to despair, never to tire of investigating the break in communication.

In particularly hardy cases of *impasse*, "controlled interruption" (Meltzer, 1968) is a technical method with which I agree, and which I have tried in a few cases. I take the opportunity of using material of particular significance to the *impasse* to suggest to the patient an interruption or—better—the suspension of therapy. I prefer total suspension, rather than just a reduction in the frequency of the sessions as Meltzer or others propose. It is essential, however, in my opinion, to make sure that the patient understands that the analyst is completely available in the future. This makes the procedure completely different from the "blackmailing" trick of the heroic expedient.

In my experience, in some cases the suggestion has the effect of focusing the project/phantasy of interminability and producing ideas about how to get out of the *impasse*. In other cases the patient agrees to the suspension and then resumes therapy some time later. It is essential, I repeat—contrary to what Freud suggests—not to make this an ultimatum, but to make sure the patient is fully aware of the analyst's availability. There are many theoretical models that underpin this technique, and the interested reader will find many referred to in Meltzer's work (1968).

I think that what happens here is somehow related to the *acte de passage* I talked about in chapter three. A very careful examination of the countertransference is needed, and full awareness of having been able to work through and overcome aggression towards the patient. Everyone recommends, in fact, that before reaching this difficult decision, we must do everything possible to work through our own emotional reactions: discussion with colleagues, possibly supervision, analysis of our own dreams, and so on. We must then make the patient realize that the aim of this operation is not just "to get rid of a difficult clinical case".

I am inclined to use the term *perversion of transference* for a series of situations closely linked with those described, but which are distinguished by some specific elements. Unlike the *impasse,* in which the conflict remains hidden for a time—sometimes even a very long time—here the conflict is openly expressed and is experienced above all in relation to the analytic setting and the analyst himself. It hinges on phantasies relating to the analytic relationship, which is felt as an intolerable primal scene (F. Meotti, 1981). We may even arrive at the creation of a fetish representing the analytic relationship, or move towards a toxicophilic tendency of the analysis (Tagliacozzo, 1980).

The patient's phantasies hinge on cheating, falsehood, obligation. The central phantasy, pivoting around the primal scene, produces the following effect: these patients are devoted to analysis and guardians of the setting, but that is because the scene has to be produced and maintained so it can be attacked and denied. We are faced with the establishment of a narcissistic illusion of self-sufficiency in the sense of being able to do without the object; this results from identification with omnipotent primal objects. But the patient needs an external object—the analyst—to sustain this illusion. The narcissistic illusion of doing without the object demands, paradoxically, the help of an external object that can be attacked and denied, thus confirming the illusion (Maldonado, 1983). In the face of the loss of this illusion, a vengeful attitude emerges, often aimed at parents, authority, and the analyst.

In the analytic scene, a game is played that offers the patient the opportunity to show that he is not a baby dependent on his parents, but quite the contrary—the parents are dependent in that they are obliged to have children, but will not then be able to bring them up.

In addition there is a basic phantasy that can be put as follows: any relationship can only be tyrannical. In these subjects, who, it seems, have not been able to accept the initial parent/

child asymmetry, there is perpetuated a phantasy of total, unshakeable asymmetry with no possibility of change.

One patient condensed his experience of this situation into an aphorism that he attributed to Mohammed: "Whoever invades the private domain of another is destined to corrupt it." In these situations, the struggle is to show that the analyst can only have a perverse purpose, verified in the patient's mind by overturning certain characteristics of the analyst at work: receptivity becomes passive masochism ("Why don't you throw me out?"), knowledge and learning become sterile erudition ("I knew this already"), neutrality and interpretation become action or violence ("What do you want of me?") (F. Meotti, 1981).

Knowledge is attacked because the prevailing emotion is fear of submission to the learning of others. Phantasies of omniscience manifest themselves through the continual feeling of knowing what is in the analyst's mind and what he feels. It is as if these subjects had theories about themselves and the analyst and expected the analyst to conform to them.

One of these patients, who showed a strong voyeuristic urge about the workings of the analyst's mind, confessed that he had often brought to the session false dreams; they were not his own but were taken from psychoanalytic books, often clinical reports by famous analysts. After his analyst had interpreted the dream, he was secretly satisfied if the interpretations appeared to him incorrect or less brilliant than those of the author of the text. He was seized with attacks of profound jealousy if the interpretations seemed similar or even better.

Another patient associated his difficulty in accepting and working through the analyst's interpretations with a particular type of behaviour of his own: he would often stop a passer-by or even a policeman to ask for information about some particularly hard-to-find city street, on which he had already done his homework, and then he enjoyed seeing the person in difficulty—or would even walk off, leaving him, saying: "Pardon me, I can see that you don't know, and I remember now that I know perfectly well myself."

In these subjects we find the phantasy that analysis is an obligation or a necessity to keep the analyst alive. This corresponds to the idea that parents are obliged to have children, just as the analyst—drugged by psychoanalysis—drugs his patients in his turn ("If you did not exist, I would not be in analysis . . . if Freud had not existed, you would not be an analyst"). This is a phantasy of a parasitic relationship of the analyst with psychoanalysis and his patients, which is matched by a similar attitude in the patient towards the analyst's mind (de Simone Gaburri, 1981).

The phantasy of self-creation is transformed into an aggressive claim to have been obliged to be born. Naturally, this situation produces phantasies of interminability or a real tendency towards interminability—in the sense that it is difficult to get out, given that the patient attacks all progress and insight that, despite everything, may be produced during the analytic work. In fact one can always feel, however weakly, the libidinal-dependent part that wants to oppose the destructive self, which is denying dependence (to use Rosenfeld's terms). Because of the idealization of the destructive self, which seems to act like a ringleader, demanding more and more crimes from its followers—the other parts of the self—the destructive part assumes seductive but tyrannical features (Rosenfeld, 1968, 1971).

This series of situations is linked to the question of *interrupted analyses.* As I have already made clear, there are no specific theoretical–clinical models for cases of so-called interminability, and even less for cases of interruption. We can only refer to the factors described so far, those preventing the analytic process from developing adequately. A situation of unshakeable resistance, or *impasse,* or repeated negative therapeutic reaction may develop with the same probability into an interruption or a tendency towards interminability.

Certain very long analyses that end because they are "worn out" (Petacchi, 1990) are, in fact, often interruptions—that is, they peter out without an adequate working-through of the conclusion. There is therefore no reason to consider an interruption more negative than certain conclusions due to wearing out, often with reciprocal idealization. On the other hand, in the post-analytic phase certain patients who have interrupted analysis speak of it later in glowing terms, and in some cases it seems that the experience of interruption was more in the analyst's mind than in the patient's.

Sometimes interruption is a "heroic expedient", this time on the patient's part, in cases where the patient does not manage to reach the analyst. To reinforce a point already made several times: we must never forget that many analyses are interrupted because of an intolerable phantasy of interminability, which has remained misunderstood and therefore not worked through.

If we leave out of consideration crude cases of actual motivation and those due to the analyst's mistakes or inexperience, every interruption must be evaluated as a case on its own in the dynamics of transference–countertransference, in order to discover the emotional situation—perhaps controllable, perhaps at that moment uncontrollable—that was at work in that situation (Gagliardi Guidi, 1992).

One technical point must be made: even if the interruption is decided by the patient, the analyst's manner of dismissal is still important. He must resist the temptation to take leave of his patient with contempt for a traitor or with the despair of a parent betrayed, or to letting his bitterness turn to hate. This would not be helpful for either party (Gesuè, 1992). Better, if appropriate, to make it understood that the analyst is always available; the patient will decide whether to benefit from this in the future or to transfer to another analyst, in either event to everyone's advantage.

Readiness to see not only the negative side of interruptions appears quite frequently in the analytic literature. Rangell (1966) considered it appropriate in certain cases to suggest an interruption, subsequently waiting until therapy could be resumed under better conditions. I would like to draw attention once more to the technique of controlled interruption, in cases of *impasse*, of which I spoke earlier.

CHAPTER FIVE

What should we think of "Analysis Terminable and Interminable" today?

Several times in the preceding chapters I have found myself citing Freud's "Analysis Terminable and Interminable" (1937c). Given the nature of the theme we are working on, it could not have been otherwise. But now we must look at it in greater detail, standing beside Freud, as it were, and taking an overall view of the work.

After tackling the theoretical and technical questions, we come back to the initial question: is analysis terminable? How, and in what sense?

This is why I have not put this chapter at the beginning of the book, which might have seemed more logical. "Analysis Terminable and Interminable" is one of Freud's most widely cited and fascinating works, besides being one of his last, and it can be looked upon as a sort of spiritual testament. However fascinating it is, none of us today would agree with all of it. We all feel, though—as Tagliacozzo said on this very subject of Freud's last writings—that Freud's heritage does not consist only of a body of doctrine that enables us to interpret so many mental happenings; above all, it has taught us a very special way of making our minds work (Tagliacozzo, 1990). That is why Freud's writings—even if we cannot always accept all he says—continually open new ways to reflect on mental facts and events.

But in "Analysis Terminable and Interminable" there is more, and I believe it is the intuition of genius reflected in the title. I feel, in fact, that the meaning of the title is not about deciding which analyses can be terminated and which not, but about singling out, within any analysis, which elements can be concluded and which cannot—or must not—reach an end. Even today, this work is one of the most powerful stimuli we have, making us reflect on the "limit" and turning point of each analysis, but also on the inexhaustible possibilities for new transformations.

The term "interminable" should thus not be taken only in the pessimistic sense of something that cannot be concluded, but also in the positive sense of acquisitions that are always open and renewable. The expression "terminable/interminable" comprises an intuition of the continuous/discontinuous nature of the analytic process. Many such opposing pairs have been proposed to help define a subject as multifaceted as this: analyses that are finished and unfinished, possible and impossible, speakable and unspeakable, and so on. Freud's attitude in this work, which may appear pessimistic, has been widely dissected (Meltzer, 1978; de Simone, 1990c).

Freud spoke as though psychoanalytic technique and theory had reached such a level as to allow an almost definitive overall evaluation, instead of considering it still in its infancy, with ample space for far-reaching change.

Freud was afraid of the technical and theoretical innovations of some of his pupils. In some cases his doubts were well founded, but elsewhere he displays an almost incomprehensible blind spot, as in the case of his refusal to take into consideration the discoveries relating to the psychoanalysis of children and psychotics, discoveries that were already outstanding at that time.

With the re-proposal of the duality of the instincts, excessive value came to be given to economic factors.

Freud was greatly preoccupied with the analysis of future analysts. In fact, he expressed himself in dramatic terms (Freud, 1937c):

> It seems that a number of analysts learn to make use of defensive mechanisms which allow them to divert the implications and demands of analysis from themselves (probably by directing them onto other people), so that they themselves remain as they are and are able to withdraw from the critical and corrective influence of analysis. Such an event may justify the words of the writer who warns us that *when a man is endowed with power it is hard for him not to misuse it*. [italics added; the "writer" is Anatole France, in his work *La révolte des anges*]

I have often wondered why so little emphasis has in general been laid on this passage. I believe it expresses another of those brilliant intuitions that fill this work: speaking about the personal analysis of analysts, of the danger that they may misuse the power with which they are endowed, already lays the foundations of the concept of the perverse countertransference.

Freud reaches the height of his pessimism in the last part of "Analysis Terminable and Interminable", when he speaks of the absolute limit of analysis, the bedrock against which analytic work can do nothing, particularized in penis envy or, more globally, in the repudiation of femininity. That Freud should consider the repudiation of femininity the impassable bedrock is understandable, considering that femininity is the third of the major themes Freud did not deal with, together with the psychoanalysis of children and that of psychotics.

In 1933, Freud seemed to have given up further exploration of this "dark continent", which thus remained mysterious: "If you want to know more about femininity, enquire from your own experiences of life, or turn to the poets, or wait until science can give you deeper and more coherent information." On the other hand, Freud seems confident that penis envy is not only a load-bearing structure of femininity, but also amounts to that which cannot be analysed, the insurmountable barrier, that impenetrable bedrock.

I have already attempted elsewhere a critical reflection on this passage of Freud and on the questions of envy and femininity (de Simone, 1990a, 1990c, 1992). I shall come back to just a few points. In this passage of Freud's we find, besides the integration of passivity and femininity, a certain sadomasochistic conception of sexuality and, above all, confusion between a detail of anatomy—the penis—and its symbolism. Here Freud is apparently disconsolate: "At no other point in one's analytic work does one suffer more from an oppressive feeling that all one's repeated efforts have been in vain, and from a suspicion that one has been 'preaching to the winds', than when one is trying to persuade a woman to abandon her wish for a penis . . ." (1937c).

Today we would be more likely to conclude that, because of the confusion between symbol and biology, these women were being asked to give up something quite different from a piece of anatomy—more like all their aspirations towards development and psychological completeness.

Many authors have been puzzled by Freud, at the end of his life, having recourse to biology rather than remaining faithful to the tools of analysis in order to understand a clinical difficulty and to try to see why castration anxiety—and penis envy—are so pivotal and persistent. Cooper (1987), for example, lays much stress on Freud's reluctance to tackle pre-oedipal questions, as if he had set a boundary by claiming that whatever went beyond castration anxiety could not be dealt with by psychoanalysis and was nothing but biology.

In this work Freud does not take into due account the patient–analyst relationship, and he does the same as far as the child–environment relationship is concerned when he discusses the vicissitudes of the ego and the instincts. It is the same when he looks at femininity: he seems to have a total blind spot about its socio-cultural implications, even though they had been very evident in previous works. Cooper adds that Freud does not seem to want to cast doubt on the primacy of the phallus and the principle of authority. In fact, after complaining of women's refusal to give up their wish for a penis, Freud adds the male's refusal to accept a passive position in relation to another man, here, too, confusing dependence with submission. There is an implicit demand that patients should submit to his authority, and Cooper notes that Freud seems to treat this as a fact, rather than as a phantasy to be analysed.

At this point, then, we find ourselves faced with a clinical theoretical model that Freud could not give up, and a technical requirement—that women patients should let themselves be convinced—necessary for the validation of that theory.

Barande (1968), commenting on Freud's work, wonders whether we are dealing with a biological law or a countertransferential fact, and he notes that interminability, or the limits of analysis, might be related to the analyst's desire to achieve a result fitting in with a theoretical presupposition; this is, so to speak, related to the difficulty of distancing oneself from one's own theories, or even ideologies. In a discussion of some points of view on bisexuality and femininity, I found myself (de Simone, 1992) comparing the last part of "Analysis Terminable and Interminable" with a passage from Winnicott's work "Creativity and its Origins" (1971), in the section "The Split-Off Male and Female Elements to be Found in Men and Women". The two passages illustrate the rigid application of theories, as opposed to a subtle and transformative use.

Winnicott, in his clinical description, speaks of a mature, socially successful man, treated by various analysts for some decades. Winnicott sensed that there was something the patient could not manage to express, which was what brought him back repeatedly to analysis and prevented its conclusion. At last, one day Winnicott perceived what it was that the patient had not been able to express: the patient was talking about penis envy. He told the patient that he sounded like a girl speaking of her penis envy. Thus Winnicott and the patient could focus on why the analysis was interminable. The only conclusion the girl present in the patient could tolerate was bound up with his admission to being a girl. "The only end to the analysis that the feminine part can look for is the discovery that in fact you yourself are a girl."

Winnicott had had to take upon himself this "folly"—as he himself termed it—which was similar to that of the mother, in a previous case, who wanted to see a little girl in her boy: "Out of this we could begin to understand his conviction that the analysis could never end."

There is no need here for a theory of bisexuality or complicated countertransferential reasonings or—as Winnicott says—for new theoretical concepts or new technical principles. However, there is a radical change at the top with respect to a given theoretical model. While Freud, who cannot free himself from it, can only "preach to the wind", freedom from any reference model means that the analyst can view the patient from another angle, and the patient can "look at himself from the analyst's point of view".

These examples show how necessary it is to be continually on guard so as not to let ourselves and the patient be trapped into a false project of cure and conclusion—false because it responds mainly to some theoretical presupposition. The watchfulness is needed not only to stop anything that could inhibit and prevent the patient's growth, but also to avoid excessive claims to development.

I remember the case of a woman who had undergone repeated analytic therapy for a serious form of phobia. Fierce competition with her brothers, and the—absolutely frustrated—wish to follow them in their social success had been interpreted over and over again as penis envy. When the patient had been labelled incurable and seemed destined for interminable attempts at therapy, she started treatment with an analyst who had completely different reference models. Her wish was no longer interpreted as penis envy, and all her inhibitions about managing her own life freely and putting her own projects into action were analysed. Improvement was very evident, and she went on to enjoy great professional and social successes.

But when the conclusion of the analysis was beginning to take shape, the phobia that had been a symptom reappeared. The analyst realized that he had fallen into the same error, though in the opposite direction, as his predecessors. He had urged the patient too far along the road of social and cultural achievements—further than she could tolerate or desire. This analyst's "revolutionary" project was a *claustrum*, just as intolerable as the "reactionary" project of the patients' parents and of her previous analysts.

Having arrived at this point, how can we use the Freudian idea of the impassable, unanalysable bedrock? We all feel that there is some truth there, that in all analyses we bump into zones where, at least at that particular moment, we cannot make our way in.

Many authors have spoken of the refusal to shed omnipotence, to accept dependence, to set oneself a limit. Barande (1968) and others (Bonasia, 1988) suggested that the impassable bedrock was one's own death. Conclusion of the analysis as separation from the analyst would bring this problem to the fore. As I already said, I do not agree with this interpretive model, because I do not believe that the conclusion of the analytic process is isomorphic with the conclusion or end of life. However, as I have also specified, neither death anxiety, nor its denial, nor the refusal of dependence and difference are problems of the ending of analysis, though all or any of these questions may arise with particular vigour around that time. They are, rather, particular to the working-through of the depressive position, or to the stage when oedipal problems emerge.

I do not really believe that we can single out a defensive bedrock that is universal and structurally equal for all or some categories of persons, for all men or for all women, as Freud suggested. I am convinced that every individual has a specific personal point of his own at which he will say his own *sufficit*.

Cooper (1987) recalls that Winnicott spoke of a resistance that is due to the fact that every adult individual is an "isolate", defending himself from intrusion into his true self. He adds that patients are not grateful to us for very deep analyses, and that the most "ambitious" analyses create the greatest difficulty. I believe that there is some truth in these arguments, though the main point seems to be the "intrusion". When we speak of "intrusion", we are already outside an adequate analytic setting. *Rebus bene gestis,* in most cases the analyst and the patient know the right moment to stop.

Today it seems more that there are no strict, immutable structural facts, and that it depends on a personality as a whole and its relationships whether a given conflict will come to one conclusion rather than another, whether it will become a cause of pathology, and whether it will be able to progress within a line of development.

We find ourselves once again at the concept of *Nachträglichkeit:* the fate of whatever happened within an analytic experience or relationship will vary in relation to the existential situations that an individual encounters.

The concept expressed by Cooper, that an individual also needs to be "isolated", leads me to make a link with Berenstein's (1987) conclusions in his commentary on "Analysis Terminable and Interminable". He says:

> Analysis will approach terminability when the ego accepts the interminability of the retrospective reinterpretations of infantile events. This entails recognition of the distinctness of the object from the ego and a reduction in the narcissistic cathexis which blurs differences; a recognition that absolute knowledge is impossible, and the working through of the mental pain from this recognition; acknowledgement of the differences and the impossible boundary between the male and the female as regards knowledge of the specific pleasure of each sex; the limit to the possibilities of identification; and acceptance of *an area which cannot be shared between the ego and the object. This involves acceptance and tolerance of uncertainty open towards the future.* [italics added]

The last two points—tolerance of uncertainty towards the future and the fact that there is an area that cannot be shared—are particularly important. This latter expression may seem disconcerting, but it indicates one of the mental states necessary to arrive at a conclusion: tolerance of the fact that during and after analysis the patient may achieve some acquisitions "in solitude", without necessarily making the other take part.

The concept of the bedrock—the limit of analysability—is directly linked to the "split-off parts", or "residual conflicts", or "non-integrated parts", or "concealed nuclei" of the personality, according to the terms employed by various authors. In the last few years we have often lingered over this problem, which has been widely debated (de Simone, 1988; Eskelinen de Folch, 1991; Gaburri & de Simone, 1983; Meltzer, 1967; Sarno, 1989). Some have postulated the existence of parts of the personality that have to be kept split off and projected; mental health, they say, is based on an adequate degree of correct splitting and idealization.

On the other hand, reference is often made to Klein's final work (1958), in which, as if inviting us not to foster excessive ideals of integration, she says that the split-off parts of the self and of impulses that are rejected because they arouse anxiety and give pain may well contain valuable aspects of the personality and of the phantasy life, which is impoverished by splitting them off. Though the rejected aspects of the self and of internalized objects contribute to instability, they are also a source of artistic and intellectual inspiration.

The first point of view values stability, but also staticity. If, however, we consider the creative potential of these split-off parts, then we must take into account the possibility of continuous transformation. This is linked with the concept of "incompleteness" or "unsaturatedness", as a condition that never goes away completely, connected with original neoteny, meaning the disparity between the wish and its fulfilment.

Then there is always the third possibility: that these split-off parts or residual conflicts are preserved and manifest themselves pathologically. These conflictual elements may be manifest or latent, and their destiny and way of making themselves felt vary widely.

Freud tackles the question of "latent" conflicts in part IV of "Analysis Terminable and Interminable", using the colourful metaphor that we should perhaps let sleeping dogs lie, and that we might not even be able to wake them if we wanted to. When we find ourselves faced with a patient asking for re-analysis, it is not always easy to decide whether the conflict about which he is complaining was already present but misunderstood in the previous analysis, or whether it came on the scene afterwards. We are, however, justified in deciding that if the dogs are awakened after the conclusion of an analysis, they will be less aggressive and dangerous if they find mental functions already prepared for dealing with them.

Often an event or a conjunction of facts becomes the cause that unleashes those parts of the conflict that had remained unresolved.

A patient had successfully concluded an analytic treatment that had cured her of a severe phobia of lifts, and also considerably improved her emotional and social life; she was subsequently promoted and went to work in the United States. The first time she found herself on the ground floor of a very tall skyscraper and had to get to one of the top floors, she was seized again with intense anxiety, and she asked to take up analysis again. For these problems, too, it seems we have to turn back to the notion of *Nachträglichkeit*.

However that may be, I do not believe in the presence of split-off zones that cannot be worked through—that are "best left well alone", as we sometimes hear. There are certainly cases in which we acknowledge the inadvisability of entering certain zones of psychic experience, and some patients, in full consciousness, declare that they do not want to cross certain limits that they themselves have set. However, the analyst must always be willing to proceed in the direction of extending the mental spaces to be explored. From this point of view, if analysis as a concrete experience is terminable, then it offers interminable possibilities for experience.

Every individual has his "personal bedrock", conscious or not, and can decide to stop at it or to move around it, or to open up a passage and get beyond it. I do not believe we have the right to think of split-off zones as unanalysable forever.

CHAPTER SIX

The post-analytic phase

We have now reached the post-analytic phase, a topic that is still attracting much attention. In this chapter, we shall look closely at the post-analytic mental attitude, especially as regards self-analysis and re-analysis.

Reflection on the post-analytic phase brings us face to face with two basic questions, one theoretical and the other technical and clinical. From the theoretical point of view, we are expected to make a pronouncement on whether we extend to the period following the conclusion of analysis the specificity and dignity of a "phase of the process". Is the ending of analysis the conclusion of a process or only of a relationship? Can we really speak of a post-analytic process? What becomes of the transference/countertransference dynamics established during therapy?

Briefly, as far as the history of this concept is concerned, its official paternity can be attributed to Rangell (1966), who speaks of *post-termination*, meaning the period after the conclusion that is still part of the psychoanalytic process—his precursors include Pfeffer (1961). The concept was then fully developed by Guiard (1979), who considered the period following the conclusion as a true phase, which he calls the post-analytic process; it is a new part, with separate rights over the previous one. Guiard thus distinguishes an initial phase, a central phase of working through, and a final phase in which the patient truly becomes independent of the analyst.

From the technical point of view, it is in this last phase that we encounter the greatest difficulties in the relationship between patient and analyst, and the question arises of the analyst's mental attitude.

We have basically two "research tools" for studying the post-analytic phase: the first relies on direct, spontaneous observations by individual analysts, and the second includes all the operations that come under the heading of "follow-up studies". All sorts of new meetings may be arranged with patients: invitations by the same analyst or a different one, scheduled meetings at regular intervals, questionnaires, and so on.

This brings us to the well-known question of empirical research in psychoanalysis, an area that is certainly very interesting and likely to develop, even though it is controversial (in Italy: Conte & Dazzi, 1988; Freni, 1990; Freni et al., 1989). Numerous varied and many-faceted opinions are certain to be put forward on all the questions inherent in this subject.

The most recurrent subject of discussion is how to deal with transference neuroses and the so-called *transferential residues.* There is a rough division between those who consider that the solution of the transference is a *sine qua non* for an adequate conclusion, and those who feel that it can be put off until the post-analytic phase. Thus some analysts think that for a correct solution of the transference, changes are needed in the setting in the concluding phase, whereas others—the majority—feel that this is superfluous.

Opinions also vary about whether contacts between the patient and the analyst after the conclusion of the analysis are possible—or advisable (see Schachter, 1990, 1992). At any rate, for the time being Freni's opinion holds (personal communication, 1993):

> All studies of this type end with the need for careful follow-up studies and methods for checking the validity of treatment or reviewing the correctness of the treatment models. This should be of primary interest to analysts, given the small number of patients they can treat in their lives.

Though I look forward to the development of these studies, I personally am not in the habit of asking my patients to return after the conclusion, for catamnestic interviews; I give them to understand, however, that I am available for any new contact, if necessary. Only the patient is entitled to ask for such contacts; the analyst must abstain from promoting new contacts, though also from forbidding them. I agree with those who believe this freedom should be left to the patient. Experience teaches that patients rarely abuse this privilege.

There is no sense taking rigid positions on these plans because all analytic histories are different, in how they start and, consequently, in how they end as well. Thus the procedure each subject adopts to reorganize his life without analysis will be different. What I am about to say, therefore, comes from direct observation of my own cases and those of colleagues with whom I have been able to discuss them.

To understand what happens "afterwards", I should like to return to two of Freud's passages. The first is the famous section that concludes *Studies on Hysteria* (1895d):

> When I have promised my patients help or improvement by means of a cathartic treatment I have often been faced by this objection: "Why, you tell me yourself that my illness is probably connected with my circumstances and the events of my life. You cannot alter these in any way. How do you propose to help me, then?" And I have been able to make this reply: "No doubt fate would find it easier than I do to relieve you of your illness. But you will be able to convince yourself that much will be gained if we succeed in *transforming your hysterical misery into common unhappiness*. With a mental life that has been restored to health you will be better armed against that unhappiness." [italics added]

How can we reply today to a patient who asks the same question? Back to Freud again, in "Analysis Terminable and Interminable":

> Let us start from the assumption that what analysis achieves for neurotics is nothing other than what normal people bring about for themselves without its help.

And,

> One has an impression that one ought not to be surprised if it should turn out in the end that the difference between a person who has not been analysed and the behaviour of a person after he has been analysed is not so thorough-going as we aim at making it and as we expect and maintain it to be.

And there is more:

> Our aim will not be to rub off every peculiarity of human character for the sake of a schematic "normality", nor yet to demand that the person who has been "thoroughly analysed" shall feel no passions and develop no internal conflicts. *The business of the analysis is to secure the best possible psychological conditions for the functions of the ego; with that it has discharged its task.* [italics added].

At the end of "Analysis Terminable and Interminable", when he speaks of the strongest resistance, the "biological bedrock", Freud concludes:

> It would be hard to say whether and when we have succeeded in mastering this factor in an analytical treatment. We can only console ourselves with the certainty that *we have given the person analysed every possible encouragement* to re-examine and alter his attitude to it. [italics added].

The points brought out in these quotations re-propose in various ways the topic of the end of analysis, apparently protecting it from an idealizing attitude. This protection almost seems excessive. Certainly to achieve "the best possible psychological conditions for the functions of the ego" may seem a small step, but it can also be a very large one, depending on the level we started at. To free yourself "from neurotic misery and suffer only from common unhappiness" is no small progress—as it might seem at first sight—because neurotic misery is not easy to shake off. Certainly, you will still have to deal with common unhappiness, but you will by then have much more of a talent for benefiting from that bit of "common happiness" that may be granted you.

Dealing with a subject who has already been analysed, we must not make the mistake of interpreting all the facts of his life as though they were still linked with the early analytic process. Cooper (1987) usefully reminds us that analysis is not an event or a structure in itself "such as a work of art, which may be examined in isolation from its context". It is a piece of a patient's life, which cannot be isolated but can be examined only as "part of the patient's ongoing experience". I would add that a successful analysis is one that, as part of the life experience, manages to become integrated with the other parts making up that experience.

Freud's suggestion about freeing oneself from neurotic misery and tolerating common unhappiness is picked up by Kupers (1988) who makes it the hub of his book, *Ending Therapy*. He seeks to cast new light on the question of the duration of analysis, re-analysis, and its relationship with psychotherapy. He notes that often those who benefit from psychoanalysis come to benefit from psychotherapy and can alternate periods of psychoanalysis with periods of psychotherapy. He speaks of therapy "in pieces", and some subjects—an increasing number, according to him—show an "abstract commitment to therapy", meaning a conviction that only therapeutic intervention can ensure mental growth. Kupers also speaks of a "community of therapy consumers". This would be a "negative" community, not the type that nurtures and in some way cares for whoever belongs to it, but a community of people joined together by the secret thread of the idea that there is always a "personal cure" in prospect. The Wolf Man, with the vicissitudes of his relationship with Freud and the other analysts after him, would be in a certain sense the "progenitor" of this tendency.

According to Kupers, all this is due to the idealizing tendency surrounding the American-style self-made man and is part of a vicious circle, because analytic therapy itself is the cause of this idealization. We are returning to the fears expressed by Freud in the very first pages of "Analysis Terminable and Interminable", where he stressed the negative consequences that the ideologies connected with American "prosperity" seem to bring.

Not least, there are economic and social factors to urge one towards one or the other form of therapy, and Kupers maintains that analysts tend to be blind to these. His opinion is that when we concentrate too much on the clinical aspects and too little on a more detailed study of the psychopathological and sociocultural factors—as he thinks happens today—the result is, to paraphrase Freud, that a large part of what should be attributed simply to common unhappiness is instead attributed to psychopathology, and the therapy thus becomes interminable. Freud, who tried to draw the demarcation line between the two situations so as to prevent an army of therapists from invading the field of "common unhappiness", would, according to Kupers, have to admit failure today.

What has been said so far is certainly very important so as not to fall into the naive error of idealizing a person because he has been "analysed", but I think that we cannot stop there. If we leave absolute evaluations and get down to specific clinical situations, we find plenty of opportunities to note that, for a certain person, the analytic experience provided an opportunity to mature that no other experience could have given. To use Freud's words, a "restored mental life" must be judged in the light of the initial disturbance(s) and evaluated with respect to them.

To all this we must add the advantage an individual can derive from the knowledge of his inner world. Di Chiara (1982), on the subject of the aims of psychoanalysis, said that the knowledge of the inner world is all the more important in that it is the only reality for which an individual can be held totally responsible. He added a pathogenic hypothesis of mental disturbances: that a man who is mentally disturbed suffers from a defect of truth. Psychoanalysis would meet up with the treatment of mental disorders on this one point: that psychoanalysis would find out the truth about the inner world and would gain from the increase in this truth. Thus "having been analysed" does not mean knowing more or acquiring some particular virtue, but only—or above all—the possibility of getting in touch with one's own inner world without too much fear or constriction, and that would make it easier to increase one's capacities.

Petrella (1979), discussing the relations between the aims of treatment and psychoanalytic technique, shows clearly the two poles between which we are expected to move, the empirical and the ideal. The patient, alongside his personal myth about his origins, also carries the myth of his final redemption. The analyst, for his part, is at the same time Sphinx and therapist. The task of the analyst–Sphinx is to offer everyone apparently insoluble riddles. The task of the analyst–therapist is to let things be "articulated" in a new way, "facilitating the most favourable variants". "It is on this solution that putting into effect the 'heroic myth of everyone's everyday life which coincides with the solution of neuroses' depends."

A new myth-creating activity thus appears to be another aim of analysis. "Facilitating the most favourable variants": the expression suggests that a subject who has conducted his analysis to a satisfactory conclusion can be expected to show flexibility, a tendency not to be rigid.

Then there is the concept of "thinkability", which Tagliacozzo (1982) indicated as a goal of psychoanalysis, or the transformation of one symbolic order into another (Corrao, 1982).

All that has been said up to now is closely intertwined with another series of questions: that of the duration of analysis—which has been getting longer in the last few years—and that of re-analysis. Examining these two themes will bring us to the topic of self-analysis, which is specific to the post-analytic phase.

Many explanations have been offered for the growing duration of treatment and the tendency towards so-called "pieces" of analysis:

- the development of psychoanalytic technique and theory has pushed out the limits of analysability to include subjects who were originally excluded (psychotics, borderline, etc.);
- the possibility of analysis of the "psychotic nuclei" even in neurotic personalities makes treatment more complex and longer.

Lebovici (1980) added that the stress laid on the search for the "truth" and for knowledge of the unconscious, to the detriment of the formulation of treatment designed for therapeutic efficacy, risks widening the limits of the analytic process beyond measure. Tagliacozzo (1980) spoke of psychoanalysis as a drug, Gaskill (1980) of the myth of perfectibility, Fachinelli (1983) of "claustrophilia", Masciangelo (1985) of a "project of interminability and corruption of the Super-Ego", and many other models have been suggested. Each one has its own validity if it is applied to a certain number of cases, but none of them can be considered an all-purpose model.

In part VII of "Analysis Terminable and Interminable", when he speaks of the analysis of aspiring analysts, Freud makes his famous suggestion: "Every analyst should periodically—at intervals of five years or so—submit himself to analysis once more *without feeling ashamed of taking this step*" (italics added). There has been much discussion about this advice. Why does Freud suggest such a procedure to analysts and not to all patients? Was he worrying more, then, about analysis of analysts than patients? Was he guessing at the risk of occupational disease?

I think it is very important to stop and look at the expression "without feeling ashamed of taking this step", for both the analyst and patients. A certain emphasis on, and idealization of, the analytic process as a "complete cycle" had made many people feel ashamed to have to resort again to analysis. I think Freud wanted to exhort us to be very watchful with respect to ourselves and our behaviour in our work, but also to feel free.

I often think it would be good if an analyst could feel freer about facing the need to "submit himself to analysis once more", not because of the idea of perfectibility but for humbler and more concrete reasons—because the vicissitudes of life may have obscured his insights, and defensive states of mind, harmful to the work of analysis, may have crept in without his knowing. Of course this applies equally to patients.

Braunschweig (1980) makes an interesting suggestion when discussing the problems of re-analysis. She maintains that it is no accident that Freud speaks of an interval of five years, which is the average length of the latency period. More specifically, the interval required could be considered as that which in the theory of the *proton pseudos* separates the second event from the first. I have brought up Braunschweig's hypothesis here because it re-proposes the theme of *Nachträglichkeit*—a concept already discussed in chapter two. This concept must be kept in mind in order to understand the continuity/discontinuity that is typical of the analytic process and certainly extends into the post-analytic phase, whether or not we consider this a part of the actual analytic process.

To return now to the questions I asked at the beginning about the mental state in the post-analytic phase—these questions are all correlated and interwoven with each other: the post-analytic mental disposition, the so-called self-analytic function, and the recollection of the analysis.

We often hear it said that the destiny of an analysis is amnesia linked with that of infancy. Etchegoyen (1986) is very precise: "the destiny of a good analyst is nostalgia, absence, and in the long run oblivion". Let us re-read Freud in the "Postscript" to the case of Little Hans (1909b), when he speaks of the visit Hans, now 19 years old, paid to him:

> One piece of information given me by little Hans struck me as particularly remarkable; nor do I venture to give any explanation of it. When he read his case history, he told me, the whole

> of it came to him as something unknown; he did not recognise himself; he could remember nothing; and it was only when he came upon the journey to Gmunden that there dawned on him a kind of glimmering recollection that it might have been he himself that it happened to. So the analysis had not preserved the events from amnesia, but had been overtaken by amnesia itself.

Writing in 1938, in *An Outline of Psycho-Analysis,* Freud noted: "For a patient never forgets again what he has experienced in the form of transference, it carries a greater force of conviction than anything he can acquire in other ways." And further on: "The method by which we strengthen the weakened ego has as a starting point an extending of its self-knowledge."

Freud's two notes are only apparently contradictory: there is the memory of facts and the very special memory of the emotional experiences linked with those facts. This takes us back to the concept of "thinkability" suggested by Tagliacozzo in the sense of transformation of *mental sediments* into thoughts and creation of a *plastic contact membrane:* to Freud's concept of making the unconscious conscious is added that of making the unthought thinkable. We can even imagine, I think, *making forgetting possible.* The focal point, then, always seems to involve leaving and re-entering what Flournoy calls "secondary time", that is to say, the specific time of analytic facts that can be seen not as continuous with but as discontinuous from the normal time of life.

The mental disposition after successful analysis has thus acquired the ability to follow alternative courses to that apparently traced out originally. This is confirmed by investigators who have studied the post-analytic mental state through catamnestic research. The patient does not show a repetition of conflicts, but automatically repeats a solution learnt, while the figure of the analyst is present only in the background.

A patient who had had a long and difficult analysis because of the quality of the problems, and had put the analyst severely to the test, but who had concluded it satisfactorily, went back to the analyst to ask for advice about a relative. Speaking of his own analysis, he said that he was very satisfied, he felt very well, but he did not understand exactly why it had lasted so long. Basically, he did not remember having had such serious problems at the beginning. What could he ever have talked about for all those years? How could he have filled so many sessions? However—he added—something had remained inside him that was like a faraway experience: he felt a sort of nostalgia, though he no longer knew what for. This case shows how, despite the *forgetting,* all the emotional qualities of the experience remained.

Siracusano (1982) comes to my aid with his work "Il messaggio nascosto nell'oblio" [Message hidden in oblivion], where he says that infantile amnesia is not forgetting but "preserving in a precise and indelible way for every future way of being" and also "the strongest nostalgia originates not from remembered pleasure, but from pleasure that has been forgotten together with the experience which had generated it". Siracusano says that forgetting is only one aspect of the memory and that certain experiences demand an inexhaustible preservation, which only forgetting can give. I believe this is all closely related with the type of recollection one has of an analytic experience.

What can we say at this point about self-analysis? Classically, we speak of: (1) self-analysis in the "pure state", similar to a good capacity for introspection; (2) self-analysis in the course of analysis, which is therefore a substitute, revealing a state of narcissistic resistance to which Abraham (1919) already referred; (3) then there is the self-analysis presumed to occur in the post-analytic period after the concluding phase.

Gairinger dealt with this concept here in Italy in 1970, and her interpretation is still valid today. She maintained that the conflicts of the depressive area can be worked through again and integrated in self-analysis, but not those of the paranoid–schizoid area. Many would agree that self-analysis is something that concerns only the depressive position. This supports the conceptual scheme of a self-analytic function appearing on the threshold of the depressive position, which is reinforced and expands completely in the post-analytic phase. But this calls for a linear conception of the process, which—as I have already stressed—I do not feel I can share.

I would prefer a model on the lines of the oscillation between the paranoid–schizoid and depressive positions in which splitting operations acquire a particular positive value because they break the integration and links already made, opening up the possibility of new transformative orders (Neri et al., 1987).

Other writers deny the possibility of true self-analysis, comparable to the analytic operations involved in the patient–analyst relationship. Grinberg De Ekboir and Lichtmann (1982), for instance, have no doubt that "genuine self-analysis is impossible". They are of the opinion that self-analysis may be a sort of defensive structure that can only act in the preconscious, and its limits are proportional to the limits of the original analysis. If unresolved conflicts re-emerge, they cannot be resolved by self-analysis, and no insight is possible without an outside "interpreter".

I believe that we cannot think of self-analytic activity as automatically continuing the analytic process, as the *natural* heir to the analytic function that developed in it. However, as I said earlier, I think that the mental attitude is more likely to be flexible, automatically tending towards working through rather than action.

This leads me to make a precise technical suggestion: not to dismiss the patient with the more or less explicit task of self-analysis. It is preferable, in the concluding phases of analysis, not to stress the possibility and even less the need for subsequent self-analysis. The analyst needs to practise this kind of self-control because only the patient can decide, more or less consciously, what use to make of his analytic experience. I have listened to patients who had had analytic experiences that had come to a favourable conclusion but had nevertheless felt themselves saddled with a task of self-analysis, and who even felt guilty that they did not feel motivated, but rather tended to forget.

All this, however, does not alter the fact that numerous patients seem to avail themselves of a mental state that could be understood as self-analytic. In such cases the self-analytic tendency is just one of the possible options put into action. Certain patients remain in direct or indirect contact with their analyst for some time, or for ever. It is sometimes said that they need an analyst as a "spectator" or "supervisor" of their self-analysis.

Sometimes one has the happy experience of witnessing the emergence of those creative phenomena that Baruzzi (1987) considers specific to the final phase of successful analyses. I remember a patient who came back to the analyst to say that some time earlier she had considered the idea of taking up analysis again, and then had discovered, while reading works of literature, especially poetry, that she could find described there states of mind similar to those she herself had experienced in analysis. She had then decided to walk the two roads together: to return to reading poetry and, on this basis, to rediscover and go back over the salient points of her analysis so as to work through them again and enrich them. She considered that the real "supplement" to analysis.

At the conclusion of the analysis, then, and on the threshold of the post-analytic phase, tolerance of uncertainty is one of the functions that must be activated. As I have already said, citing Berenstein: a certain amount of uncertainty remains regarding the future of the analysis experienced, but there is the certainty that new paths have been opened that were not passable earlier, which is a further step on the way to a more precise sense of self.

The destiny of everything that has been acquired during analysis is bound up with tolerance of this uncertainty. A patient said in the concluding sessions of her analysis:

> "What will happen to what I have discovered here? Is what I have done up to now enough, or must I continue? What road shall I take? I shall say, using St John's episode of Nicodemus, 'Marvel not that I said unto thee, Ye must be born again. The wind bloweth where it listeth, and thou hearest the sound thereof, but canst not tell whence it cometh, and whither it goeth . . .' then I say to myself, let the wind blow where it wishes. . . ."

Thinking again of this patient's words, I cannot help contrasting them with those of Freud at the end of "Analysis Terminable and Interminable", when he says that "all one's repeated efforts have been in vain" and suspects that one has been "preaching to the winds" when one tries to *convince* the patients . . . and the need to stop at the bedrock.

These two opposing situations, to which I devote my final paragraphs, could have been put at the beginning as an *exergo* to indicate the two poles between which we had to travel: on the one hand a resistance apparatus, and on the other the urge towards transformation. I believe that in no other situation do we have the sense of movement that we have in an analysis that is adequately ending. The person who has begun analysis is moved partly by his own difficulties but also by the feeling that there is in fact a way out of a situation that originally looked impassable. As the conclusion of analysis is taking shape, another feeling alerts him that from the terrain of separation new paths can be glimpsed with the possibility of establishing a new balance.

Once again Freud comes to mind, speaking in 1926 of the need to substitute the reality principle for the pleasure principle. He added that the ego learns that there is yet another way of securing satisfaction for one's drives apart from an *adaptation* to the external world—that is, to intervene in the external world by changing it. But the most important thing is to integrate the two possibilities: ". . . decisions as to when it is more expedient to control one's passions and bow before reality, and when it is more expedient to side with them and to take up arms against the external world—such decisions make up the whole essence of worldly wisdom."

REFERENCES

Abraham, K. (1919). A particular form of neurotic resistance against the psycho-analytical method. In: *Selected Papers on Psychoanalysis,* London: Hogarth Press, 1954.

Balint, M. (1936). The final goal of psycho-analytical treatment. *International Journal of Psycho-Analysis, 17*: 206–216.

Barale, F., & Ferro, A. (1992). Negative therapeutic reactions and micro-fractures in analytical communication. In: L. Nissim Momigliano & A. Robutti (Eds.), *Shared Experience: The Psychoanalytic Dialogue.* London: Karnac Books.

Barande, R. (1968). L'Inachèvement de l'analyse: loi biologique ou contre transfert? *Revue Française de psychanalyse, 32*: 263–272.

Baranger, M. (1969). Regression y temporalidad en el tratamiento analìtico. *Revista de Psycoanàlisis, 26.*

Baranger, M., Baranger, W., & Mom, J. M. (1983). Process and non-process in analytical work. *International Journal of Psycho-Analysis, 68* (1): 21–35

Baruzzi, A. (1987). La fine dell'analisi. *Gruppo e Funzione Analitica, 8,* 265–278.

Berenstein, I. (1987). Analysis terminable and interminable: Fifty years on. *International Journal of Psycho-Analysis, 68* (1): 21–35.

Bezoari, M. & Ferro, A. (1992). From a play between "parts" to transformation in the couple: psycho-analysis in a bi-personal field. In: L. Nissim Momigliano & A. Robutti (Eds.), *Shared Experience: The Psychoanalytic Dialogue.* London: Karnac Books.

Bonasia, E. (1988). Death instinct or fear of death? Research into the problem of death in psycho-analysis. *Rivista di Psicoanalisi, 34* (2): 272–315.

Braunschweig, D. (1980). La demande de tranche d'analyse. *Revue Française de Psychanalyse, 44* (2): 266–274.

Conte, M., & Dazzi, N. (Eds.) (1988). *La verifica empirica in psicoanalisi.* Bologna: Il Mulino.

Cooper, A. M. (1987). Comments on Freud's "Analysis Terminable and Interminable". In: J. Sandler (Ed.), *On Freud's "Analysis Terminable and Interminable"*. New Haven, CT: Yale University Press, for the International Psychoanalytical Association, 1991.

Corrao, F. (1982). Il principio della cura. *Rivista di Psicoanalisi, 28* (4): 475–484.

de Simone Gaburri, G. (1979). Il tempo e la relazione analitica. *Rivista di Psicoanalisi, 25* (3): 340–358.

de Simone Gaburri, G. (1981). Modelli tipici di "perversione del transfert". *Rivista di Psicoanalisi, 27* (2): 205–210.

de Simone Gaburri, G. (1982a). Fantasie di interminibilità e formazione del progetto psicoanalitico. In: G. Di Chiara (Ed.), *Itinerari della psicoanalisi.* Turin: Loescher.

de Simone Gaburri, G. (1982b). Il tempo dell'analisi fra sintomo e conoscenza. *Rivista di Psicoanalisi, 28* (4): 540–547.

de Simone Gaburri, G. (1984). L'esperienza del tempo in psicoanalisi. *Quaderni di Psicoterapia Infantile, 10*: 110–116.

de Simone Gaburri, G. (1985). On termination of the analysis. *International Review of Psycho-Analysis. 12* (4): 461–468.

de Simone Gaburri, G. (1988). On the subject of post-analysis. *Rivista di Psicoanalisi, 34* (2): 244–270.

de Simone Gaburri, G. (1990a). Il concetto psicoanalitico di invidia. In: G. Pietropolli Charmet & M. Cecconi (Eds.), *L'invidia: aspetti sociali e culturali.* Milan: Scheiwiller.

de Simone Gaburri, G. (1990b). Further considerations on the conclusion of analysis. *Rivista di Psicoanalisi, 36* (2): 340–368.

de Simone Gaburri, G. (1990c). Some observations on "Analysis Terminable and Interminable" and on the concept of envy. *Rivista di Psicoanalisi, 36* (4): 862–876.

de Simone Gaburri, G. (1992). On femininity. Some notes on the "Inhibition of thought". *Rivista di Psicoanalisi, 38* (2): 472–488.

Di Chiara, G. (1978). La separazione. *Rivista di Psicoanalisi, 24* (2): 258–269.

Di Chiara, G. (1982). Sulla finalità della psicoanalisi: il significato delle costruzioni nell'analisi. In: G. Di Chiara (Ed.), *Itinerari della Psicoanalisi.* Turin: Loescher.

Di Chiara, G. (1990). Preface. In: H. Thomä & H. Kächele, *Trattato di Terapia Psicoanalitica, Vol. 1.* Turin: Bollati Boringhieri.

Di Chiara, G. (1991). Tradizione e sviluppi nella teoria e nella clinica psicoanalitica. Alcune considerazioni sul processo analitico. Read at the first Italian–German Colloquium, Loveno di Menaggio, 8 June.

Di Chiara, G. (1992). Meeting, telling and parting: three basic factors in the psychoanalytic experience. In: L. Nissim & A. Robutti (Eds.), *Shared Experience: The Psychoanalytic Dialogue*. London: Karnac Books.

Eskelinen De Folch, T. (1987). The obstacles to analytical cure: Comments on "Analysis Terminable and Interminable". In: J. Sandler (Ed.), *On Freud's "Analysis Terminable and Interminable"*. New Haven, CT: Yale University Press, for the International Psychoanalytical Association, 1991.

Etchegoyen, R. H. (1986). *The Fundamentals of Psychoanalytic Technique*. London: Karnac Books, 1991.

Fachinelli, E. (1979). *La freccia ferma. Tre tentativi di annullare il tempo*. Milan: L'Erba Voglio.

Fachinelli, E. (1983). *Claustrofilia*. Milan: Adelphi.

Ferenczi, S. (1927). The problem of termination of the analysis. In: *Final Contributions to the Problems and Methods of Psychoanalysis*. London: Hogarth Press, 1955.

Ferrara Mori, G. (1993). Sogni predittivi della psicoanalisi. Read at the Centro Psicoanalitico di Firenze, 10 June.

Ferro, A. (1993). The impasse within a theory of the analytical field: possible vertices of observation. *International Journal of Psycho-Analysis, 74* (5): 817–929.

Flournoy, O. (1979). *Le temps d'une psychanalyse*. Paris: Belfond.

Flournoy, O. (1985). *L'acte de passage*. Neuchâtel: A la Baconnière.

Freni, S. (1990). Lo Junktim freudiano alla luce degli attuali orientamenti di ricerca empirica in psicoanalisi. Read at the Centro Milanese di Psicoanalisi, 22 March.

Freni, S., Marinetti, M., Pasquali, G., & Tognoli, L. (1989). I fattori terapeutici attraverso un questionario: risultati e considerazioni. *Rivista di Psicoanalisi, 35* (2): 244–287.

Freud, S. (1895d) (with Breuer, J.). *Studies on Hysteria*. *SE 2*.

Freud, S. (1909b). Analysis of a phobia in a five-year-old boy. *SE 10*.

Freud, S. (1912e). Recommendations to physicians practicing psychoanalysis. *SE 12*.

Freud, S. (1916–17). *Introductory Lectures on Psycho-Analysis*. *SE 10*.

Freud, S. (1926e). *The Question of Lay Analysis*. *SE 20*.

Freud, S. (1933a). *New Introductory Lectures on Psycho-Analysis*. *SE 22*.

Freud, S. (1937c). Analysis terminable and interminable. *SE 23*.

Freud, S. (1940a). *An Outline of Psycho-Analysis*. *SE 23*.

Gaburri, E. (1987). La fine dell'analisi fra fatto scelto e fatto compiuto. Read at the Meeting, "Conflitti residui, strategie e tecniche del lavoro dello psicoanalista", Rome, 5–8 May.

Gaburri, E., & de Simone Gaburri, G. (1982). L'emergenza del bello e la relazione analitica. In: G. Di Chiara (Ed.), *Itinerari della psicoanalisi.* Turin: Loescher.

Gaburri, E., & de Simone Gaburri, G. (1983). Idealizzazione e narcisismo nella relazione tra il Sè e gli oggetti. *Rivista di Psicoanalisi, 29* (2): 243–262.

Gagliardi Guidi, R. (1992). Premature termination of analysis. In L. Nissim Momigliano & A. Robutti (Eds.), *Shared Experience. The Psychoanalytic Dialogue.* London: Karnac Books, 1992.

Gairinger, L. (1970). L'autoanalisi. *Psiche, 7* (1): 75–87.

Gaskill, H. S. (1980). The closing phase of the psychoanalytic treatment of adults and the goals of psychoanalysis—the myth of perfectibility. *International Journal of Psycho-Analysis, 61* (1): 11–23.

Gesuè, A. (1992). La cerimonia degli addii, una riflessione sulle analisi che si interrompono. *Rivista di Psicoanalisi, 38* (3): 687–725.

Grinberg, L., Langer, M., Liberman, D., de Rodrigué, H., & de Rodrigué, G. (1967). The psychoanalytic process. *International Journal of Psycho-Analysis, 48*: 496–503.

Grinberg, L. (1980). The closing phase of the psychoanalytic treatment of adults and the goals of psychoanalysis: "The search for truth about oneself". *International Journal of Psycho-Analysis, 61* (1): 25–37.

Grinberg De Ekboir, J., & Lichtmann, A. (1982). Genuine self-analysis is impossible. *International Review of Psycho-Analysis, 9* (1): 75–83.

Guiard, F. (1977). Sobre el componente musical del lenguaje en etapas avanzadas y finales del anàlisis. Consideraziones técnico-clinicas y metapsicologicas. *Revista de Psicoanàlisis, 34*: 25–76.

Guiard, F. (1979). Aportes al conocimiento del proceso post-analàtico. *Psicoanàlisis, 1*: 171–204.

Klauber, J. (1977). Analysis which cannot be terminated. *International Journal of Psycho-Analysis, 58*: 473–477.

Klein, M. (1950). On the criteria for the termination of a psycho-analysis. In: *The Writings of Melanie Klein, Vol. 3: Envy and Gratitude and Other Works,* ed. by Roger Money-Kyrle, Betty Joseph, Edna O'Shaughnessy, & Hanna Segal. London: Hogarth Press, 1975 [reprinted London: Karnac Books, 1991].

Klein, M. (1958). On the development of mental functioning. In: *The Writings of Melanie Klein, Vol. 3: Envy and Gratitude and Other Works,* ed. by Roger Money-Kyrle, Betty Joseph, Edna O'Shaughnessy, & Hanna Segal. London: Hogarth Press, 1975 [reprinted London: Karnac Books, 1991].

Kupers, T. A. (1988). *Ending Therapy: The Meaning of Termination.* New York: New York University Press.

Laplanche, J., & Pontalis, J.-B. (1967). *The Language of Psycho-Analysis.* London: The Hogarth Press, 1973 [reprinted London: Karnac Books, 1988].

Lebovici, S. (1980). La fin de l'analyse et ses modes de terminaison. *Revue Française de Psychanalyse, 44* (2): 235–283.

Le Guen, C. (1982). L'Après-coup. *Revue Française de Psychanalyse, 46* (3): 527–534.

Liberman, D., Barrutia, A., Issaharoff, E., & Winograd, B. (1985). Indicadores del finál del análisis. In: *Homaje a David Liberman. APdeBA, 7* (1–2): 159–173.

Lipton, S.D. (1961). The last hour. *Journal of the American Psycho-Analytical Association, 9*: 325–330.

Maffei, G. et al. (Eds.) (1992). La conclusione dell'analisi. *Rivista di Psicologia Analitica, 46.*

Maldonado, J. (1983). Compromiso del analista en el impasse psicoanalitico. *Revista de Psicoanàlisis, 40*: 205–218.

Marramao, G. (1991). Dibattito su "Minima Temporalia" di Giacomo Marramao, with F. Corrao, G. Marramao, D. Meghnagi, & L. Russo (edited by G. Nebbiosi). *Koinos—Gruppo e Funzione Analitica, 12* (1): 46–72.

Masciangelo, P. M. (1985). Analyse, réanalyse et interminabilité. In: *Psychanalyse.* Neuchâtel: A la Baconnière.

Meltzer, D. (1967). *The Psychoanalytical Process.* London: Heinemann.

Meltzer, D. (1968). Una tecnica de interruption de la impasse analitica. In: Leon Grinberg (Ed.), *Prácticas psicoanalíticas comparadas en las neurosis.* Buenos Aires: Paidós, 1977.

Meltzer, D. (1978). *The Kleinian Development, Vol. 1: Freud's Clinical Development.* Perthshire: Clunie Press.

Meotti, A. (1991). I fini dell'analisi in una prospettiva storica. Read at the first Italian–German Colloquium, Loveno di Menaggio, 8 June.

Meotti, F. (1981). Su alcune dinamiche fra paziente e analista nel transfert perverso. *Rivista di Psicoanalisi, 27* (2): 198–204.

Modell, A. H. (1990). *Other Times, Other Realities: Toward a Theory of Psychoanalytic Treatment.* Cambridge, MA, & London: Harvard University Press.

Neri, C. (1990). Keeping alive. In: C. Neri, L. Pallier, G. Petacchi, G. C. Soavi, & R. Tagliacozzo, *Fusionalità. Scritti di psicoanalisi clinica.* Rome: Borla.

Neri, C., Correale, A., & Fadda, P. (1987). *Lettere bioniane.* Rome: Borla.

Nissim Momigliano, L. (1974). Come si originano le interpretazioni dell'analista. *Rivista di Psicoanalisi, 20*: 144–185.

Nissim Momigliano, L. (1979). Taccuino d'appunti. *Rivista di Psicoanalisi, 25*: 178–198.

Nissim Momigliano, L. (1992a). Two people talking in a room: An investigation on the analytical dialogue. In: L. Nissim Momigliano & A. Robutti (Eds.), *Shared Experience: The Psychoanalytic Dialogue.* London: Karnac Books.

Nissim Momigliano, L. (1992b). Continuity and change in psychoanalysis. *Letters from Milan.* London: Karnac Books.

Petacchi, G. C. (1990). Analisi di logoramento. In: C. Neri, L. Pallier, G. Petacchi, G. C. Soavi, & R. Tagliacozzo, *Fusionalità. Scritti di Psicoanalisi.* Rome: Borla.

Petrella, F. (1979). Rapporti tra la finalità della cura e la tecnica della psicoanalisi. *Gli Argonauti, 1* (1): 25–36.

Pfeffer, A. (1961). Follow-up study of a satisfactory analysis. *Journal of the American Psychoanalytical Association, 9*: 698–718

Quinodoz, J. M. (1991). *The Taming of Solitude. Separation Anxiety in Psychoanalysis.* London & New York: New Library of Psychoanalysis, 1993.

Rangell, L. (1966). An overview on the ending of an analysis. In: R. E. Litman (Ed.), *Psychoanalysis in the Americas—Original Contributions from the First Pan–American Congress for Psychoanalysis.* New York: International University Press.

Rickmann, J. (1950). On the criteria for the termination of analysis. *International Journal of Psycho-Analysis, 31*: 200–211.

Ricoeur, P. (1983). *Time and Narrative.* Chicago, IL: University of Chicago Press, 1984–1988.

Riolo F. (1986). Il Processo analitico: una revisione del modello. *Rivista di Psicoanalsi, 32* (3): 389–404.

Rosenfeld, H. (1968). Notes on the negative therapeutic reaction. Read to the British Psycho-Analytical Society.

Rosenfeld, H. (1971). A clinical approach to the psychoanalytic theory of the life and death instincts: an investigation into the aggressive aspects of narcissism. *International Journal of Psycho-Analysis, 52* (2): 169–178.

Russo, L. (1991). Dibattito su "Minima Temporalia" di Giacomo Marramao, with F. Corrao, G. Marramao, D. Meghnagi, & L. Russo (edited by G. Nebbiosi). *Koinos—Gruppo e Funzione Analitica, 12* (1): 27–41.

Sacerdoti, G. (1986). Riflessioni sulla bipolarità inerenti al processo psicoanalitico con particolare riguardo alla continuità/discontinuità. *Rivista di Psicoanalisi, 32* (2): 195–208.

Sarno, L. (1984). Il setting psicoanalitico fra costituzione interna e migrazioni istituzionali. II. Sulla separazione. *Prospettive analitiche nel lavoro istituzionale, 2* (1): 132–146.

Sarno, L. (1989). Sull'interminabilità analitica e sulla "tecnica" della fine analisi. *Koinos—Gruppo e Funzione Analitica, 10* (3): 15–28.

Schachter, J. (1990). Post-termination patient–analyst contact: I. Analysts' attitudes and experience; II. Impact on patients. *International Journal of Psycho-Analysis, 71* (3): 475–486.

Schachter, J. (1992). Concepts of termination and post-termination patient–analyst contact. *International Journal of Psycho-Analysis, 73* (1): 137–154.

Siracusano, F. (1982). Il messagio nascosto nell'oblio. *Rivista di Psicoanalisi, 28* (3): 320–328.

Tagliacozzo, R. (1980). Psicoanalisi come droga—Note sul progetto e sulla terminabilità dell'analisi. *Rivista di Psicanalisi, 26* (3): 307–316

Tagliacozzo, R. (1982). La pensabilità: una meta della psicoanalisi. In: G. Di Chiara (Ed.), *Itinerari della Psicoanalisi.* Turin: Loescher.

Tagliacozzo, R. (1990). Trying to think with Freud. *Rivista di Psicoanalisi, 36* (4): 804–828.

Thomä, H., & Kächele, H. (1985). *Psychoanalytic Practice, Vol. 1: Principle,* 1987; *Vol. 2: Clinical Studies,* 1988. Berlin: Springer Verlag.

Thomä, H., & Cheshire, N. (1991). Freud's Nachträglichkeit and Strachey's "deferred action": trauma, constructions and the direction of causality. *International Review of Psycho-Analysis, 18* (3): 407–427.

Ticho, E. (1972). Termination of psychoanalysis: treatment goals, life goals. *Psychoanalytic Quarterly, 41*: 315–333.

Usuelli Kluzer, A. (1989). Il contratto perverso. In: A. Semi (Ed.), *Trattato di Psicoanalisi, Vol. 2.* Milan: R. Cortina Editore.

Usuelli Kluzer, A. (1992). Il tempo nell'analisi: punti di vista sulla interminabilità. Read at the Fourth Italian–French Meeting, Lyons, November.

Winnicott, D. W. (1962). The aims of psycho-analytical treatment. In: *The Maturational Processes and the Facilitating Environment: Studies in the Theory of Emotional Development.* London: Hogarth Press and The Institute of Psycho-Analysis, 1965 [reprinted London: Karnac Books, 1990].

Winnicott, D. W. (1971). Creativity and its origins. In *Playing and Reality.* London: Tavistock.

Wittgenstein, L. von (1931). Notes on Frazer's Golden Bough. In: Klagge & Nordmann (Eds.), *Philosophical Occasion, 1912–1951.* Indianapolis, IN, & Cambridge: Hackett, 1993.

BIBLIOGRAPHY
OF WORKS OF GENERAL INTEREST

Chapters one and three

The most complete bibliographical and critical study I have found in the last few years appeared in the monothematic issue of the *Rivista di Psicologia Analitica, 46* (1992), Astrolabio, Rome, entitled "La conclusione dell'analisi", edited by G. Maffei. Under the title "Symposia", this contains symposia, colloquies, meetings, panels, and reports of congresses, starting with the Marienbad Congress in 1936, on the subject of the termination of analysis.

For the theoretical, clinical, and technical aspects, see R. H. Etchegoyen, *The Fundamentals of Psychoanalytic Technique*, chapters 46–48 (London: Karnac Books, 1991).

Thorough reviews on the subject can also be found in H. Thomä & H. Kächele, *Psychoanalytical Practice, Vol. 1: Principle* (Berlin: Springer Verlag, 1987); T. A. Kupers, *Ending Therapy: The Meaning of Termination* (New York: New York University Press, 1988); J. M. Quinodoz, *The Taming of Solitude. Separation Anxiety in Psychoanalysis* (London & New York: New Library of Psychoanalysis, 1993).

See also: A. Saraval, "La tecnica classica e la sua evoluzione", in A. A. Semi (Ed.), *Trattato di Psicoanalisi, Vol. 1: Teoria e Tecnica*, Chapter 8 (Milan: R. Cortina, 1988).

I would like to draw attention to the monographic issue of the *Revue Française de Psychanalyse* (no. 2, 1980), entitled, "La fin de la cure psychanalytique", with articles by Lebovici, Braunschweig, Gaskill, Firestein, and the French translation of Grinberg's paper, "The Closing Phase of the Psychoanalytic Treatment of Adults and the Goals of Psychoanalysis: 'The Search for Truth about Oneself'". *International Journal of Psycho-Analysis, 61* (1, 1980): 25–37.

Chapter two

A useful review of the literature on time in different disciplines can be found in the single volume, "Temporalità", *Koinos—Gruppo e Funzione Analitica* (no. 1, 1991).

For a collection of works by classical authors, see A. Sabbadini (Ed.), *Tempo in Psicoanalisi* (Milan: Feltrinelli, 1979).

Note also Number 10 of the *Quaderni di Psicoterapia* (1984), entitled "Tempo e psicoanalisi", and the monothematic issue of the *Nouvelle Revue de Psychanalyse, 41* (1990), entitled "L'Epreuve du temps".

For discussions on the concept of the analytic process, see Etchegoyen, op. cit., and Thomä & Kächele, op. cit.

For the explanation of *Nachträglichkeit,* I suggest A. H. Modell, *Other Times, Other Realities* (Cambridge, MA: Harvard University Press, 1990) and, in French, the monothematic issue of the *Revue de Psychanalyse* (no. 3, 1982), entitled "L'Après-coup", which contains, among others, a work by Claude Le Guen.

Chapter four

For factors that impede the analytic process, it is worth looking at chapters 52–60 of Etchegoyen, op. cit. See also the Panel on "La perversione del transfert", *Rivista di Psicoanalisi* (no. 2, 1981).

Note also D. Meltzer, *Sexual States of Mind* (Perthshire: Clunie Press, 1973).

For the concept of the negative therapeutic reaction, see M. Arrigoni Scortecci, "La reazione terapeutica negativa", and A. Giannotti & S. Grimaldi, "La reazione terapeutica negativa", both of which appear in *Rivista di Psicoanalisi, 33* (1987).

For good bibliographical information on the works of Herbert Rosenfeld, see the bibliography to *Shared Experience,* edited by L. Nissim Momigliano & A. Robutti (London: Karnac Books, 1992).

Chapter five

Rivista di Psicologia Analitica, 46 (1992), cites the Panels and Congresses that have had as their theme "Analysis Terminable and Interminable". I would recommend the Colloquies of the Paris Psychoanalytic Society (1966), "En relisant en 1966 'Analyse terminée et analyse interminable'", published in the *Revue Française de Psychanalyse 32* (1968), with interventions by R. Barande and J. Chasseguet-Smirgel, among others.

I also advise reading the papers given at the Montreal Congress: "Analysis Terminable and Interminable 50 Years Later", published in the *International Journal of Psychoanalysis* (1987–1988); and J. Sandler (Ed.), *On Freud's "Analysis Terminable and Interminable"* (New Haven, CT: Yale University Press, for the International Psychoanalytical Association, 1991).

Note also F. Fornari, "A proposito di 'Analisi terminabile e interminabile'", in *Simbolo e codice* (Milan: Feltrinelli, 1976); and "L'idée de guérison", in *Nouvelle Revue de Psychanalyse* (no. 17, 1978).

Chapter six

The reader interested in the question of follow-up studies will find an exhaustive treatment of the subject in the *Rivista di Psicologia Analitica, 46* (1992), in the paper "Postanalisi e follow-up studies".

In addition to the works of Schachter cited in chapter six, I would call attention to the following:

Panel, 1987: "Evaluation of Outcome of Psychoanalytic Treatment: Should Follow-up by the Analyst be Part of the Post-Termination Phase of Analytical Treatment?" *Journal of the American Psychoanalytical Association, 37* (1989): 813–822 (fall meeting of the American Psychoanalytic Association, New York, 19 December 1987: chairman, J. Schachter; reporter, M. Johan).

J. L. Kantrowitz et al., "Follow-up of Psychoanalysis Five to Ten Years after Termination. I. Stability of Change", *Journal of the American Psycho-Analytical Association, 38* (1990): 471–496; "II. Development of the Self-Analytical Function", ibid.: 637–654; and "III. The Relation between the Resolution of the Transference and the Patient–Analyst Match", ibid.: 655–678.

N. Schlessinger & F. Robbins, "Assessment and Follow-up in Psychoanalysis", *Journal of the American Psycho-Analytical Association, 22* (1974): 542–567; and *A Developmental View of the Psychoanalytic Process. Follow-up Studies and Their Consequences* (New York: International Universities Press, 1983).

R. S. Wallerstein, *Forty-Two Lives in Treatment: A Study of Psychoanalysis and Psychotherapy* (New York: Guilford Press, 1986).

H. M. Bachrach, J. J. Weber, & S. Murray, "Factors Associated with the Outcome of Psychoanalysis" (Report of the Columbia Psychoanalytic Center Research Project: IV), *International Review of Psycho-Analysis, 12* (1985): 379–389.

J. J. Weber, J. Elinson, & L. M. Moss, "The Application of Ego Strength Scales to Psychoanalytic Clinic Records", in G. S. Goldman & D. Shapiro (Eds.), *Developments in Psychoanalysis at Columbia University* (New York: Hafner, 1966).

INDEX

TOWARDS LILLERS*

In October, marching taking the sweet air,
Packs riding lightly, and home thoughts soft coming,
'This is right marching, we are even glad to be here,
Or very glad?' But looking upward to dark smoke foaming
Chimneys on the clear crest, no more shades for roaming,
Smoke covering sooty what men's heart holds dear,
Lillers we approached, a quench for thirsty frames,
And looked once more between houses and at queer names
Of estaminets, longed for cool wine or cold beer.
This was war, we understood; moving and shifting about;
To stand or be withstood in the mixed rout
Of fight to come after this. But that was a good dream
Of justice or strength-test with steel tool a gleam
Made to the hand. But barb-wire lay to the front,
Tiny aeroplanes circled as ever their work
High over the two ditches of heart-sick men;
The times scientific, as evil as ever, again.
October lovely bathing with sweet air the plain.
Gone outward to the east and the new skies
Are aeroplanes, and flat there as tiny as bright
As insects wonderful coloured after the night
Emerging lovely as ever into the new day's
First coolness and lucent gratefulness
Of the absorbing wide prayer of middle sight
Men clean their rifles insentient at that delight
Wonder increases as fast as the night dies.

Now up to the high above aeroplanes go
Swift bitter smoke puffs and spiteful flames,
None knows the pilots, none guesses at their names,
They fly unthought courses of common danger,
Honour rides on the frame with them through that anger,
As the heroes of Marathon their renown we know.

* The *London Mercury*, Vol. XXIX, No. 170, December 1933.

OLD DREAMS*

Once I had dreamed of return to a sunlit land,
Of summer and firelight winter with inns to visit,
But here are tangles of fate one does not understand,
And as for rest or true ease, where is it or what is it?

With criss-cross purposes and spoilt threads of life,
Perverse pathways, the savour of life is gone.
What have I then with crumbling wood or glowing coals,
Or a few hours' walking, to work, through a setting sun.

I SAW FRENCH ONCE*

I saw French once—he was South Africa cavalry
And a good leader and a successful, clever one to me.
A knight of Romance—for the knight of Veldt was about him
Who outwitted Boers—few could—who laid traps and got him.
Egypt and Aldershot—Commander of the Forces
And Mons Leader—and Ypres of the Worcestershires.
Now Captain of Deal Castle—so my book advises.
We were paraded for six mortal long hours of shoulders strain
And after hours of cleaning up of leather and brasses—
(O! never, never may such trial be on soldiers again!)
And it was winter of weather and bitter chill,
Outside of Tidworth on a barren chalk slope—Wiltshire Hill
Six long hours we were frozen with heavy packs—
Brasses cleaned bright, biscuits in haversacks.
At last horses appeared hours late, and a Marshal
Dismounted, our shoulders so laden we were impartial
Whether he shot or praised us—Whether France of the Line
Or soft fatigues at Rouen or Abbeville or Boulogne.
Slow along the ranks of stiff boys pained past right use
Egypt and Veldt—Ulster—Mons, Ypres came

* The *London Mercury*, Vol. XXIX, No. 17, December 1933. *Poems of Ivor Gurney*, 1954.

And none to shout out of Ypres or cry his name—
Hell's pain and silence gripping our shoulders hard
And none speaking—all stiff—in the knifed edged keen blast.
He neared me (Police used electricity) Ypres neared me
The praises of Worcestershires, Joffre's companion Captain he
Who the Médaille Militaire the soldier known of France wore,
Scanned me, racked of my shoulders, with kind fixed face
Passed, to such other tormented ones, pain-kept-in-place
To stare so—and be satisfied with these young Gloucesters
Who joined to serve, should have long ago seen Armentières,
As Ypres, but at least Richebourg or near Arras.
But they would not send—youth kept us rotting in a town
Easy and discipline worried—better by far over by Ovillers—
Or Béthune—or St Omer—or Lys, Scrape, those rivers
To keep a line better than march by meadow and down.
Chelmsford army training to bitterness heart turning
Without an honour—or a use—and such drear bad days
Without body's use, or spirit's use—kept still to rot and laze,
Save when some long route march set our shoulders burning
Blistered our heels—and for one day made body tired.

Anyway, on the chill slope we saw Lord French, Commander on the hill
Of short turf, and knew History and were nearer History
Soon for scarred France—to find what Chance was to be feared,
To leave those damned Huts and fall men in shell blast and shots.
To live belt-hungry—to freeze close in narrow cuts
Of trenches—to go desperate by barbed wire and stakes
And (fall not) keep an honour by the steel and the feel
Of the rifle wood kept hard in the clutch of the fingers, blood pale

The coming of French after freezing so long on the slope.
Tidworth was Hell—men got Blighties—at least equal hope.
This was March—in May we were overseas at La Gorgue—
And the Welshmen took us, and were kind, past our hoping mind—
Signallers found romance past believing of War's chance.
But the leader of Mons we had seen, and of History a mien,
South Africa and the first days, Mons, Ypres and between.

CHRISTOPHER MARLOWE*

With all that power he died, having done his nothing . . .
And none of us are safe against such terrible proving
That time puts on men—Such power shown—so little done . . .
Then the earth shut him out from the light of the sun.
All his tears, all his prayers to God, and Elizabethan loving
Gone to a nothing, before he was well of age—
Having seen Cornwall, perhaps visited a loved Germany,
Known all London, read in many a poet's page—
Brave and generous, braggart and generous in doing,
Poet born and soldier, sobering to his elder age;
The earth covered him, and wrought wood was his clothing.
'Tamburlane' half glorious, the 'Faustus', half victorious,
He left us, chief, an ache that a poet true of men,
Should be stabbed cold, like any mean half gallant frothing
nothing
Other men honoured, great ones made a tradition true,
But we curse luck for silence in manner various—
The courage and youth and virtue of Christopher Marlowe.

WHEN THE BODY MIGHT FREE†

When the body might free, and there was use in walking,
In October time—crystal air-time and free words talking
In my mind with light tunes and bright streams ran free,
When the earth smelt, leaves shone and air and cloud had glee.

Then there was salt in life but now none is known
To me who cannot go either where the white is blown
Of the grass, or scarlet willow-herb of past memory.
Nothing is sweet to thinking from life free.

* *Poems of Ivor Gurney*, 1954.

† 1. The *London Mercury*, Vol. XXIX, No. 171, January 1934. 2. *Poems of Ivor Gurney*, 1954.

WHEN MARCH BLOWS*

When March blows, and Monday's linen is shown
On the gooseberry bushes, and the worried washer alone
Fights at the soaked stuff, meres and the rutted pools
Mirror the wool-pack clouds, and shine clearer than jewels.

And the children throw stones in them, spoil mirrors and clouds
The worry of washing over; the worry of foods
Brings tea-time, March quietens as the trouble dies . . .
The washing is brought in under wind-swept clear infinite skies.

DRACHMS AND SCRUPLES†

Misery weighed by drachms and scruples
Is but scrawls on a vain page.
To cruel masters we are pupils,
Escape comes careless with old age.

O why were stars so set in Heaven
To desire greedily as gluttons do;
Or childish trinkets—may Death make even
So rough an evil as we go through.

EARLY SPRING DAWN‡

Long shines the thin light of the day to north-east,
The line of blue faint known and the leaping to white;
The meadows lighten, mists lessen, but light is increased,
The sun soon will appear, and dance, leaping with light.

* The *London Mercury*, Vol. XXIX, No. 171, January 1934.
† The *London Mercury*, Vol. XXX, No. 178, August 1934.
‡ *Poems of Ivor Gurney*, 1954.

Now milkers hear faint through dreams first cockerel make crow,
Faint yet arousing thought, soon must the milk pails be flowing;
Gone out the level sheets of mists, and the West row
Of elms are black on the meadow edge, Day's dear wind is blowing.

THE TOUCHSTONE*

What Malvern is the day is, and its touchstone—
Gray velvet, or moon-marked; rich, or bare as bone;
One looks towards Malvern and is made one with the whole;
The world swings round him as the Bear to the Pole.

Men have crossed seas to know how Paul's tops Fleet,
That as music has rapt them in the mere street,
While none or few will care how the curved giants stand,
(Those upheaved strengths!) on the meadow and plough-land.

ROADS—THOSE ROADS*

Roads are sometimes the true symbolical
Representations of movement in the fate of man.
One goes from Severn of tales and sees Wales
A wall against England as since time began.

Hawthorn and poplar call to mind the different people
That rule and had shaping of this land at their periods.
One goes from the Abbey to the smaller steeples,
There made worthy, and by tithe-barns, and all by roads.

* *Poems of Ivor Gurney*, 1954.

Daylight colours gray them, they are stained blue by the April
Skies on their pools and Summer makes carpet of dust
Fit for the royal; Autumn smothers all with colour
Blown clean away by the withering cruel Winter's gust.

Roads are home coming and a hope of desire reached,
(There is the orange window at the curve of the dark way),
Whether by Winter white frozen or by Summer bleached,
Roads are the right pride of man and his anxiety.

FEBRUARY DAWN*

Rooks flew across the sky, bright February watched
Their steady course straight on, like an etcher's line scratched.
The dark brown or tawny earth breathed incense up,
I guessed there were hidden daisies, hoped the first buttercup.

The tunes of all the county, old-fashioned and my own
Wilful, wanton, careless, thronged in my mind, alone
The sight of earth and rooks made passion rise in my blood,
Far gleamed Cotswold. Near ran Severn. A god's mood.

Save that I knew no high things would amaze day fall
I had prayed heaven to kill me at that time most to fulfil
My dreams for ever. But looked on to a West bright at five,
Scarred by rooks in purpose; and the late trees in strife.

* *Poems of Ivor Gurney*, 1954.

A MADRIGAL*

Trees, men, flowers, birds, nuts, sing one choir
One madrigal shout far: scatter clouds with brass:
Scholars, leave your book folded, run, follow here,
Harvest is done, the year's high set in flower . . .
Michael and his armed press, Raphael, all chivalry here,
Echo beat the tympan of the woods, cry all clear—
Blast, bray, bellow deep sounds for the Master of the Year.

GENERATIONS*

The ploughed field and the fallow field
They sang a prudent song to me;
We bide all year and take our yield
Or barrenness as case may be.

What time or tide may bring to pass
Is nothing of our reckoning,
Power was before our making was
That had in brooding thought its spring.

We bide our fate as best betides
What ends the tale may prove the first
Stars know as truly of their guides
As we the truth of best or worst.

* *Poems of Ivor Gurney*, 1954.

I LOVE CHRYSANTHEMUMS*

I love chrysanthemums and winter jasmine
Clustering lichened walls a century old,
Ivied windows that the sun peeps in
When dawn an hour gone sees the level gold.
But for my love, Sweet William, snowdrops, pansies,
To else she is cold.

And all the host of tiny or mighty things
Scattered by April, daring autumn frost.
Or of man's hand scarcely her imaginings
Touch, being save to these three careless almost
And save to me. This knowing should I envy
Princes of proudest cost?

EPITAPH ON A YOUNG CHILD

They will bury that fair body and cover you—
You shall be no more seen of the eyes of men,
Not again shall you search the woodlands—not ever again
For violets—the wind shall be no more dear lover of you.

Other children shall grow as fair, but not so dear.
And the cold spirited shall say 'It is wrong that the body
Should be so beautiful'—O puritans warped to moody!
You were the true darling of the earth of your shire.

And all the flowers you touched, but would for pity not pick,
In the next Spring shall regret you and on and so on—
Whether you are born again your love shall not be done—
In the most wonderful April or October your spirit shall be
mystic.

* *Poems of Ivor Gurney*, 1954.

Dear body (it is an evil age) that so enclosed
So lovely a spirit, generous, quick to another's small pain:
Is it true you in the dark earth must be down-lain?
Are there no more smiles from you in the house, sunlight drowsed?

I must find out a love to console my hurt loneliness,
Forget your children's beauty in the conflict of days—
Until there come to me also the sweetness of some boy's
Or girl's beauty—a Western spirit in a loved coloured dress of
flesh.

POEM FOR END*

So the last poem is laid flat in its place,
And Crickley with Crucifix Corner leaves from my face
Elizabethans and night-working thoughts—of such grace.

And all the dawns that set my thoughts new to making;
Or Crickley dusk that the beech leaves stirred to shaking
Are put aside—there is a book ended; heart aching.

Joy and sorrow, and all thoughts a poet thinks,
Walking or turning to music; the wrought out links
Of fancy to fancy—by Severn or by Artois brinks.

Only what's false in this, blood itself would not save,
Sweat would not heighten—the dead Master in his grave
Would my true following of him, my care approve.

And more than he, I paid the prices of life
Standing where Rome immortal heard October's strife,
A war poet whose right of honour cuts falsehood like a knife.

War poet—his right is of nobler steel—the careful sword—
And night walker will not suffer of praise the word
From the sleepers; the custom-followers, the dead lives unstirred.

Only, who thought of England as two thousand years
Must keep of today's life, the proper anger and fears,
England that was paid for by building and ploughing and tears.

* *Poems of Ivor Gurney*, 1954.

THE HOE SCRAPES EARTH*

The hoe scrapes earth as fine in grain as sand,
I like the swirl of it and the swing in the hand
Of the lithe hoe so clever at craft and grace,
And the friendliness, the clear freedom of the place.

And the green hairs of the wheat on sandy brown.
The draw of eyes toward the coloured town,
The lark ascending slow to a roof of cloud
That cries for the voice of poetry to cry aloud.

SONNET TO J. S. BACH'S MEMORY†

Honoured Sebastian, that to many men
Has been the speaker of their deep honour—
You that have kept makers in fine manner
Beyond any, save Shakespeare—here again
One writes to praise thee; and for the Christian
Greatness, thy nobleness of strict banner,
Of grey metal, of truth of love's demeanour—
Page on page with the look and life of stone—

Europe gives thanks ennobling, Sebastian,
When Her heart touches thy praise. It is Her own
Hard and age-old virtue, out of prayer grown.
The aisles that fill with thunder, the height that thrills,
Most to thy name respond. And it is predestined
That by the chief gratitude men will make miracles.

* *Music & Letters*, Vol. XIX, No. 1, January 1938.

† 1. *R.C.M. Magazine*, Vol. XXXIV, No. 2, 1938. 2. Reprinted in the *Daily Telegraph*. This reprint differed in some details from Gurney's own version because the Music Editor altered the grammar. (Note by M. M. S.)

THE SONGS I HAD*

The songs I had are withered
Or vanished clean,
Yet there are bright tracks
Where I have been,

And there grow flowers
For other's delight.
Think well, O singer,
Soon comes night.

WHEN I AM COVERED*

When I am covered with the dust of peace
And but the rain to moist my senseless clay,
Will there be one regret left in that ill ease

One sentimental fib of light and day—
A grief for hillside and the beaten trees?
Better to leave them, utterly to go away.

When every tiny pang of love is counterpiece
To shadowed woe of huge weight and the stay
For yet another torment ere release

Better to lie and be forgotten aye.
In Death his rose-leaves never is a crease.
Rest squares reckonings Love set awry.

* 1. *Music & Letters*. Vol. XLX, No. 1, January 1938. 2. *Poems by Ivor Gurney*, 1954.

INDEX OF FIRST LINES